IN WEAKNESS, STRENGTH

books by Jean Vanier
published by Griffin House

IN WEAKNESS, STRENGTH (1969)
TEARS OF SILENCE (1970)
ERUPTION TO HOPE (1971)
BE NOT AFRAID (1975)

books *about* Jean Vanier's work

MY BROTHER MY SISTER (1972)
revised edition 1974
L'ARCHE JOURNAL (1973)

IN WEAKNESS, STRENGTH

the spiritual sources of

General The Rt. Hon. Georges P. Vanier, P.C., D.S.O., M.C., C.D.

19th Governor-General of Canada

by his son

Jean Vanier

GRIFFIN HOUSE

Toronto 1975

© Jean Vanier, 1969, 1975

ISBN o 88760 073 5

Published by Griffin Press Limited

461 King Street West, Toronto M5V 1K7 Canada

First Published 1969

Second Printing 1969

First Published in paper covers 1971

Second Printing 1972

Third Printing 1973

First Published in this format 1975

Printed and bound in Canada by

T. H. BEST PRINTING COMPANY LIMITED

DEDICATION

This book is dedicated to the memory of my father and to my mother who shared his life.

It was written with the help of my sister and brothers.

We thank all those who made its publication possible and especially George Cowley.

CONTENTS

FOREWORD

All who admired, respected and loved the late Georges Vanier
will welcome Dr. Jean Vanier's glimpses into the secret of
his father's greatness. Here it will be clear "that the spiritual
side of his life was the very source of his greatness in public matters".

It is left to the official biographer to describe this man of many
parts. As lawyer, soldier, diplomat, ambassador and, for over seven
years, Canada's Governor General, Georges Philias Vanier had various careers and lived a full life, often arduous, frequently under
stress, sometimes extremely dangerous. Yet those who saw him in
action, carrying out the duties which increasing responsibilities
thrust upon him, testify to his inner serenity, his unshakable courage,
his transparent honesty, his refreshing common sense and his delightful sense of humour.

This book opens the door to the pathway which led him to the
acquisition and development of such characteristics. Above all, it
helps us to understand how one who was "every inch a man" could
demonstrate so clearly a tenderness and sensitivity in his relations
with all sorts and conditions of men. People of all kinds found in
him a living example of Charles de Foucauld's ideal of "universal
brother". For him, the pathway was the way of prayer. His scale of
priorities gave primacy to the spiritual. "We feel," says the author,
speaking for his family, "that his spiritual life, his life of prayer
and of spiritual reading, was not just a *part* of his existence . . .
but was the very *source* of all his motivations. . . ."

This account of a spiritual pilgrimage is remarkable for its
restraint. The son of one who had undertaken important responsibilities in the service of his country, and who had been granted
its highest honour, might well have used his own remarkable gifts
of expression to portray his father's virtues and abilities. He does
not do so. Instead, he gives us here vignettes of the impressions

General Vanier made on others, some insights into his inner struggles as shown in private jottings and leads us to see what became the ruling passion of his life, namely to work "that God's will may be done".

One little incident which spoke volumes about the character of the man and of his sense of the spiritual occurred a few days before he was to be installed as Governor General of Canada on September 15, 1959. General Vanier made a hurried trip from Montreal to Ottawa. He wanted, as a private citizen, to make some visits in the Capital in a way in which protocol would soon prevent him doing. I remember his telephone call to my office. Could he come around for a few moments to "pay his respects," as he put it. "Don't go to any bother, I should like to call on you just as you are," he added. We chatted for about half an hour. Just as he was about to leave, I told him that our Church had regular prayers for those who occupied the post of Governor General, and that I should now be thinking of him at these times. His face immediately lit up as he told me how much he valued prayer. "What we need," he said, "is sufficient strength for the day, as it says in the 'Our Father", 'Give us this day our daily bread.' " It was said quite naturally, with no apparent break from what we had previously been discussing. The next seven years, provided so many examples of this easy transition from "ordinary affairs" to the deep things of the spirit.

At some point in his life, Georges Vanier learned that if a man wants to find God everywhere, he must find Him somewhere. As a devout Roman Catholic, this began for him at Mass. Describing a deepening of his father's spiritual experience in 1938, Dr. Vanier writes: "He began to take Communion every Sunday and shortly afterwards expressed a desire to accompany my mother every morning to Mass. From this time on, except, of course, when exceptional circumstances absolutely prevented him from doing so, he decided to live each day under the signs of Christ's love and to seek the communion of His Flesh and Blood." Here he found the Presence which went with him into all the concerns of life.

Such spiritual discipline can become a boring or a dry routine. As one who loved life, General Vanier must have experienced such temptations. If so, he managed to overcome them. The book helps us to see his method. It shows one who simply loved God and wanted to grow in that love. Spiritual exercise was just as necessary for that growth as is training for any other kind of development. He added to attendance at Mass and participation in Holy Communion a daily period of quiet meditation. Humble enough to recognize that we can learn from others in this field as in others, he sought the direction of spiritual masters. This book introduces us to some of those whom he found helpful.

This book has a universal appeal. It not only describes the inner life of one who found, as did Dag Hammarskjöld, that "In our era, the road to holiness necessarily passes through the world of action," but provides for our day of activism a clue to the sanity, the integrity and the wisdom without which human life has no meaning.

It was this blend of action and meditation, of activity and quiet which gave a delightful naturalness to Vanier's piety. Everyone knew he was intensely interested in human beings, always wanting to serve human need and one who would go to infinite pains to be of help. Such a disposition, coupled to heavy schedules of official duties inevitably meant long and full days. These were saved from mere busyness by the daily practice of prayer and meditation which he and his gracious wife kept inviolate. Official ceremonies were saved from emptiness and formal meetings rescued from tediousness by the inner strength, the warmth of love and the quality of balance which came from such times of quiet renewal.

General Vanier was a true ecumenist. He knew and valued his own religious tradition. He cherished the best that he knew it to possess. Unashamedly and loyally he practised what that tradition taught. Yet always he respected the religious heritage of others. He was open to what other traditions had to give. Time and time again, as Governor General, he made it clear that he would welcome opportunities to worship in churches other than his own. Always one felt that such participation was more than that of an official discharging the duties of his office, but was the offering of worship of one who lived so close to God that he could find Him not only in the religious ceremonies he loved but in any others sincerely presented.

If "reverence for the Eternal is the source of wisdom," then this book illustrates how one who lived fully, loved greatly, served nobly—and with it all, was a delightful human—came to find it. It also portrays one who found in life the truth of the prophet's insight that "they who wait upon the Lord shall renew their strength."[1]

Ernest S. Reed,
Bishop.

Ottawa,
May, 1969.

[1] Isaiah, 40:31.

When Georges Philias Vanier died on March 5th, 1967, the extent of the sorrow expressed throughout Canada astonished even those who knew him best. Some 36,000 people filed past to pay their final tribute as his body lay in state in the Senate. From every corner of the world flowed countless messages of sympathy.

On the morning of his funeral a whole nation paused in its daily activities and there was hardly a newspaper or radio station in the country which did not devote much of its space or time to his passing. There were those who said that never before in the history of Canada had one man's death evoked so universal a reaction, or united, if only for a moment, the infinite diversity of our country in the common cause of remembrance and reflection.

No one would have been more surprised at how nearly universal was this reaction than the Governor-General himself. We, his children, and those others who knew him best would have expected much more than he this widespread feeling of loss, but even we would not have guessed how far the influence of so modest and unassuming a person had permeated.

In many ways his greatness must be an enigma to anyone who lacks spiritual sensitivity. He was an intelligent man, it is true, and was graced with the common sense to know his own limitations, but he was not, by any stretch of the imagination, a great intellectual.

After an excellent record in studies in Montreal and at Laval University, he passed his bar examinations for the Province of Quebec and spent three years practising law with a large firm. He worked with complete conscientiousness, but without attracting the least attention. A dedicated and courageous soldier, an able and perceptive diplomat, he nonetheless did not have the genius that marks the real maker of history in these fields. In each of his many careers he could best be described as competent and conscientious.

He was subject to many of the shortcomings of temperament and personality that handicap us all. He was not half French and half Irish for nothing, and his reactions could be quick and angry. Physically, quite apart from the growing handicap that the loss of a leg imposed upon him, he was in his later years frail, and suffered from heart and other ailments.

But yet so many felt attracted to him, warmed by his very presence. Not intellectually or scientifically great, he was however deeply endowed with qualities of the will and of the heart. His professional life was marked by scrupulous honesty; honesty in word and in deed; never exaggerating in any way and having a horror of anything that might smack of abuse of power. He was in many ways a living example of him whom the Bible and the ancients called the "just man", the man of duty: duty to his family, to his country, to his God. His motto might well have been: "I seek but to serve".

But these qualities of justice and honesty do not by themselves explain the warmth of goodness that radiated from him. Many who wrote about him at the moment of his death spoke of another, even more impressive characteristic. They used the term "love". Hugh Kemp said on the Canadian Broadcasting Corporation:

"He loved us—openly, and we loved back'."[1]

Catherine Doherty wrote:

"It was by his love of all of us, which somehow escaped in utter simplicity and approachability, that he was able to bring God closer to us . . ."[2]

My father had a public life which one could call fully successful: he reached the highest position in his country, he was honoured and esteemed by all. But he had as well a spiritual life, an inner life hidden in many regards even from his family. His outward success was not unrelated to this inner life; on the contrary, we are convinced that the spiritual side of his life was the very source of his greatness in public matters. Certainly it made him particularly sensitive to the needs and feelings of others: it added to his remarkable moral rectitude a radiant warmth which won the affection of all who knew him. It is precisely to try to illu-

[1] Radio Canada, March 8, 1967.
[2] Catherine Doherty, *Restoration*, Combere, Ontario, April 1967, Volume XX, p. 4.

minate these inner sources of his outer strength that we have written these pages.

These few pages are necessarily inadequate and above all incomplete. But may it not be better, in such matters, to indicate paths rather than attempt a complete assessment too rapidly after his death. We felt that those who knew him and loved him should be allowed to know more of the inner life from which he drew his strength, while his memory was still fresh in their hearts.

But in many ways we have misgivings. He himself was so discreet concerning his private and interior life that it might seem better to maintain this same discretion, keeping these pages only for the family circle and his most intimate friends.

His deep respect for others was the source of his discretion concerning his own faith. He did not want to preach and above all he feared wounding others. He did not wish to impose his personal beliefs and he was the last to think others less good because they did not share them.

Having decided to speak of his spiritual life we would like to do so in the same spirit as my father's discretion, wishing simply to indicate for those who loved and admired him some of the lights and loves that guided him.

Instead of devoting a separate book to the spiritual insights of my father, we could have encompassed them in a larger biography. The spiritual side of his life would thereby be placed in its broader context, a context which would have made clear the ways in which his love was expressed for his family, his friends, his regiment, and for his country and its two cultures. But the risk would have been to drown the spiritual in a flood of details.

We feel that his spiritual life, his life of prayer and of spiritual reading, was not just a *part* of his existence, even the most noble, but was the very *source* of all his motivations, of his love and tenderness, of his sense of duty and integrity, of his desire to serve.

A volume dedicated to his spiritual qualities has the advantage of bringing to the fore his more profound motivations, thus showing more clearly the rôle that his Christian beliefs played in his personal and public life. But, we realize we may give the impression that he was in some way "disincarnate", separated from us all by spiritual experiences that most of us, men and women of the twentieth century, cannot even hope to attain, that he was, in short, a model that none could imitate. We have chosen, however, to run this risk, because those who knew him even slightly know well how close he was to us all; far from being "disincarnate" he was con-

3

cerned with all human activities, interested in everything around him, and especially sympathetic to the rising generation; he had his simple joys, his quick sense of fun, his deep sense of duty, just as he had his faults and his temper, and his *a priori* judgements, which were the products of his early education and his background.

His character was formed by an upbringing which stressed love of tradition, but he was nonetheless a man of his time, open and receptive to the most modern currents of thought.

Obviously, like all of us, he struggled between the pull of a traditional way of life and thought and the new ideas and forms of expression which have so marked our modern world. His humility and his openness helped him to resolve these conflicts.

This book makes no claim to be a biography. A work of that nature is at present being written by Mr. Robert Speaight. But many persons have told us how much they hope that a separate project such as this will be undertaken to throw some light on the spiritual life they suspected existed in my father.

It is with a great feeling of inadequacy that we publish these pages. Others could have done better. We apologize to those who loved him and who would have expected a more complete work. All we wish is that some of his simplicity and humility, his love and respect for all men flowing from his personal love and experience of Jesus Christ may permeate these pages, without in any way exaggerating or making of him a person remote or intangible.

"I was glad when they said to me 'Let us go to the house of the Lord'"

No one at Government House suspected, on Saturday the 4th of March, 1967, that the Governor General would die the following day. True, he seemed tired and often short of breath. It had been for this latter reason that the doctors had advised him to take oxygen. Wearing his face mask, he looked, as one of the Aides said to him, as if he had just arrived from outer space. "No," he replied without a second's hesitation, "I am just leaving for outer space!" Did he himself realize that his departure was imminent?

That Saturday evening he watched, as always, the hockey match and was happy to see his favourite team "Les Canadiens" of Montreal win their match. After the game was over, he asked to be wheeled to the Chapel, and there he stayed for some time, as he did every night, close to the altar in the presence of God.

4

The next morning when my mother entered his room she realized as soon as she touched his hand that something was wrong. He seemed even weaker than usual. When his physician, Dr. Peter Burton, arrived at 9:30 a.m. for his daily visit, he saw that my father was dying. He was peaceful and drowsy and in no way showed signs of anxiety.

Towards 10 a.m. his faithful chaplain, Chanoine Guindon[3] gave him Holy Communion, while my father quietly recited three times the words called for in the liturgy, "Lord, I am not worthy that Thou shouldst enter under my roof; say but the word and my soul shall be healed." The regular service of Mass of Rideau Hall was due to begin in a few minutes in the Chapel next door and my father, noticing the clock beside his bed, reminded us that it was time we went to the service.

It was there, in the room next to his, that we recited together the words of Psalm 122 which form the opening prayer of the Mass of the fourth Sunday in Lent: "I was glad when they said to me, 'Let us go to the house of the Lord!'" We spoke these words with tears in our eyes, but our hearts were in peace. We knew that the time had come for my father to enter into the joy of his Heavenly Father.

After Mass we returned to his room. Chanoine Guindon administered the last rites, and peacefully he breathed his last breath, no agony, just a deep peace which permeated us all. Thus he died as he had lived, in extreme simplicity, no drama, no last words, just in silence and peace. Around his bed, we remained in that same silence and peace.

But the serenity with which he died had not been achieved without sacrifice. Barely forty-eight hours before his death, he had submitted his resignation as Governor General, giving in to the urgings of his doctors. How dearly, however, would he have liked to stay on in office, to be able to open the great world's fair, Expo '67 in Montreal, and to represent the Canadian people, the people he loved so deeply; he spoke often of the heads of state whom Canada would welcome during the celebration of its centennial year, and in particular did he discuss with satisfaction the preparations being made for the visit of General de Gaulle. The verdict of his doctors came to him as a sign of the will of God. He accepted this sign and his heart was at peace, in spite of the considerable uncertainty he must have felt concerning his own personal future.

[3] Chanoine Guindon was the chaplain at Rideau Hall during my father's term of office. He himself, died a few months after my father's death.

5

Doctor Paul David,[4] his cardiological specialist, made the following testimony about my father's last days in a letter here translated from the French, which the doctor wrote to my mother in July of 1967:

"His abandonment to the will of God gave him a rare serenity and real interior peace. His main desire on a human plane was to serve his country for as long as possible. . . . I have the impression that during the last six months of his life your husband waged a battle, the intensity and depth of which few realize.

In September 1966, the signs and symptoms of cardiac insufficiency worsened and required more intensive treatment. A few weeks later, an urgent operation was carried out without any serious complications. However, in spite of prolonged rest, the cardiac insufficiency persisted. Thus began 1967, centennial year, the year of Expo.

As the details of the official program for the first months of Expo became known, Dr. Burton and I became increasingly worried by the evident incapacity of our patient. How could he possibly carry out all these obligations?

We suggested that he increase his activity each day and take his meals downstairs in the dining room. These steps seemed essential in trying to evaluate the possibility of further physical effort. They would also allow your husband to realize his limitations. After three weeks of this régime the situation was still uncertain. And so, in agreement with your husband and yourself we decided to call in Dr. Paul Dudley White of Boston.

After careful examination of the patient and of the situation, Dr. White failed to see how the Governor General could meet his obligations. With the greatest kindness and tact, Dr. White explained the situation to your husband. The next morning, as we left, the General admitted: 'My friends, you are right. I accept your verdict. For some time I have felt the almost intolerable weight of the efforts I have to make.' And he added: 'May I ask you one favour? That of receiving, as arranged, a group of students from the University of Montreal. I would like to keep the appointment. I will deliver to them, I promise you, my last speech as Governor General . . .'

[4] Dr. Paul David is President of the American Society of Cardiology and founder of the Montreal Cardiological Institute.

Your husband kept his word. He informed the Prime Minister of his decision to retire. He spoke to the students. Two days later, during the Mass of Laetare Sunday (Sunday of Joy), he died, very peacefully.

As a Catholic heedful of such signs, I had the impression that your husband's 'yes' to the medical verdict was required by Providence. The 'yes' of abnegation and detachment was apparently necessary. Was death, three days later, only coincidence?

For seven years, we had the privilege of receiving certain confidences. We are certain that your husband had reached a summit reserved for a few exceptional human beings. In truth, your husband lived with God and by God. The presence of God was expressed in his gestures and words, with, of course, the utmost discretion and disarming simplicity. Is holiness anything other than this intimate and constant life with God? The ultimate acceptance of the medical verdict by your husband seemed to me the sign awaited by God who then took him to his reward."

If he approached death without fear—and I am sure that he wanted above all to spare us any worry—it was because of his certainty in life after death. His faith was deep. During the last few months of his life he read mainly the New Testament, the Gospels and the Epistle of St. Paul. His life was one of service to God and to his fellow-men, and his death was not an end but merely a beginning of life in the presence of God.

"Georges Vanier died as he lived, said Cardinal Léger.[5] He had agreed to the extension of his tour of duty so that he might open the world fair. It was an inspiration on the Government's part to ask him to stay on. But even as he accepted this final call in the service of his country, the Governor General knew that his weak heart would have to make a supreme effort. It is therefore no exaggeration to say that he died on the field of honour. He was faithful to his first calling right to the end. Old soldiers pass from us surrounded by a halo of glory. But he was also faithful to the very end to his calling of a Christian, of one who has been baptised."

[5] Cardinal Leger, Homily at the Governor General's funeral mass, the Basilica, Ottawa, March 8, 1967.

"From all evidence, he was a man who walked with God"[6]

But one might well ask whether my father had always known the peace and serenity of which we have spoken, or whether they were not rather the results of a lifetime of self-discipline and slow spiritual progress. If we examine his life story it is easy enough to ascertain two major milestones in the evolution of his interior life, milestones which he had first to pass before reaching the road to this inner peace.

It seems certain that my father possessed a genuine faith from the days of his early childhood. And as a youth he had already a keen sense of duty, a scrupulous and sensitive conscience, and an absolute honesty. We might say perhaps that his faith was governed by a certain Jansenist spirit, that is that it was influenced more by a sense of fear than love. He never once missed attending Mass on Sundays, but he sought communion only two or three times a year, and then only immediately after having made his confession, for fear that he might otherwise be in an insufficient state of purity to receive his Lord. We know, too, that during the First World War he went out of his way to try to dissuade soldiers from swearing (see page 51). But there can be no doubt that his spiritual development, however firmly it was based, had not in his youth begun to flourish, handicapped as it was by this element of fear outweighing the importance of love.

Nonetheless, from the time of his marriage, little by little certain changes became evident. The serenity which was a characteristic of my mother's spiritual life could not fail to help inspire a common desire on both their parts to deepen their interior life. Feeling the need for guidance in her spiritual development, my mother liked, moreover, to seek the advice of those who had achieved an intense prayer-life, persons such as Father Steuart, a Jesuit preacher whom she heard for the first time in 1933 in England. Throughout most of the 1930's, my parents lived in London, where my father was Secretary at the office of the Canadian High Commissioner, Vincent Massey. It was, however, only in 1938 that my father also had occasion to hear Father Steuart. It was one day early in spring of that year that he happened to be leafing through his newspaper and noticed that the Scottish Jesuit would be preaching on Good Friday. "Did you know that your Father Steuart will be speaking at a church quite close to us?" he asked

[6] "Georges Vanier" by Robert Speaight, *The Tablet*, March 8, 1967.

my mother. "I would love to hear him," she replied, "won't you come with me?" Feeling perhaps a bit trapped, my father somewhat reluctantly agreed. At the service itself, Father Steuart spoke with great simplicity and yet great depth about the love manifested by a God who was willing to sacrifice his own Son for men's salvation. My mother still remembers that when it came time to leave the church she noticed that my father was sitting there as if completely overcome. He met Father Steuart in person shortly afterwards and told him that his sermon had inspired him to change the entire direction of his life. For the first time, he declared, he began to realize just how intense was God's love for man. From that moment on his spiritual life progressively deepened and a new sense of communion arose between my parents, elements which formed the foundation of their life together and allowed them to help each other further along the road of spiritual development.

He began to receive communion every Sunday, and shortly afterwards expressed a desire to accompany my mother every morning to Mass. From this time on, except of course, when exceptional circumstances absolutely prevented him from doing so, he decided to live each day under the signs of Christ's love, and to seek the communion of His Flesh and Blood. My mother has told me how, after his escape from France in 1940 (where he had been Canadian Minister in Paris), throughout the bombing of London and right on to his service as Canadian representative with General de Gaulle at Algiers and afterwards, he spared no effort to attend Mass every day, in spite of the frequent physical strain which such an effort imposed upon him. If, occasionally, he was unable to attend a regular service, he would arrange for my mother and himself to receive communion privately.

It is thus not surprising that when later he was named to the position of Governor General, my mother and he thought at once of establishing a chapel at the Viceregal residence in Ottawa, where Mass could be celebrated daily. This chapel, situated near his bedroom, became in a way the centre of the house. Never once did he pass the chapel door without opening it and bowing in adoration before the altar. Never would he undertake any important function without coming first to the chapel to ask for the guidance of the Holy Spirit. Often he would enter the small room simply to seek spiritual refreshment.

"It is my hope that very shortly," he wrote in a letter dated just after his installation as Governor General, "we will have an altar where Christ the King will reign. To Him will I give the keys of my house, to him will I cede my place, Him will I ask to occupy my throne and allow me to serve at His feet."

In addition to his daily attendance at Mass and his frequent visits to the chapel, my father, as did my mother, felt the need to dedicate at least half an hour of every day to personal and silent prayer. What factors led him to set aside this daily half-hour of prayer? It was a habit which both my parents followed carefully since the time of my father's appointment as Ambassador in Paris in 1944. Of the many influences upon my parents, perhaps the most significant were derived from the books of Father Boylan[7], and from personal contact with a Dominican priest and a Carmelite nun who had been a great friend of my mother for many years. My father cherished the privilege of writing to her because he recognized in her a person very united to God. It was both through this nun and through my mother, who had herself been long attracted by the spirituality of the Carmelites, that my father came to know the writings of St. John of the Cross and of St. Teresa of Avila.

He loved reading Father Boylan, and he read many of his books a number of times as the following extract from a letter to a Cistercian Abbot testifies, written on the 9th of March, 1964, shortly after the death of Father Boylan.

> "Although I never had the pleasure of meeting him, I knew him well through his spiritual writings, all of which I have read, in some cases more than once. I feel I owe it to his memory and to myself to put on record this tribute of deep gratitude. It all began curiously enough by my reading in the French version *Difficulties in Mental Prayer* which I picked up at a Carmel in Paris. That was the beginning of an important change in my life."

The decision of my eldest brother to enter the Cistercian Order of the Trappist Monks in 1946 confirmed—if I may use this expression—my father's attraction to the spirit of Saint Bernard, founder of the order which he had first come in contact with through Father Boylan.

It is interesting to note that my father, who had such an active public life, over-charged with official demands, had an inner life which developed through the inspiration of the writings of the mystics, of monks and of nuns dedicated to cloistered lives of contem-

[7] Father Boylan was Abbot of a Trappist Monastery in Ireland and wrote among others, *The Spiritual Life of the Priest, Difficulties in Mental Prayer, This Tremendous Lover.*

plation. It was as a result of these writings that my parents decided to consecrate a certain portion of each day to silent prayer. In Paris, they often went together in the Embassy car with their long-time chauffeur, Monsieur Fromaget, to the small church on rue Cortambert to undertake what they soon began referring to as their "half-hour".

This thirty minutes became a part of the day that was virtually sacred. Never would my parents let either fatigue or other pre-occupations come between them and this regular meeting with their Saviour. It was not surprising that my father underlined the following passage in one of Father Boylan's books:

> "There is no use arguing about it, you are going to be asked to give an hour daily to reading, reflection and prayer no matter how busy you are. No man is too busy to eat, neither is any man too busy to feed his soul."[8]

So convinced was he of the wisdom of Father Boylan's words that if events conspired to prevent him completing his "half-hour" during the day, he would insist on doing so before retiring. How often do we remember entering his room to wish him goodnight and finding him sitting quietly in a chair or in bed, his hands folded. With a word or a gesture, he would let us know that he was in the midst of his time of prayer and would be grateful if we would postpone our visit until he was finished.

And yet this rigorously allotted time of prayer was evidently sometimes dry and difficult for him. We noticed him on more than one occasion looking at his watch to see if the time was up. Never did we see him with a book. Usually, he would simply sit in silence before the altar. At other times, he was obviously in deep peace and meditation. But whether in dryness and distraction or in peace and recollection, he would always remain faithful to the divine rendez-vous that he had made.

We know very little of the content of this time he spent with his Lord. Did he just remain in front of the altar expressing actively but in silence his faith and love for Jesus, or did he remain in passive but loving abandonment seeking simply that Jesus possess him more and more? None can say. Here we touch the mystery of the secret relations between man and his Creator. My father spoke very little about these times of prayer. We have only a few hints, the passages he underlined in his books and some notes scribbled

[8] Father Boylan, *The Spiritual Life of the Priest*, p. 16, Mercier Press, 1949.

on odd bits of paper which we found scattered among his personal papers after his death.

Some of the spiritual notes were written in French and others in English. It seems evident that they were written on the spur of the moment, but nonetheless with considerable care. They are not written in the style of a diary or formal record, and it seems most unlikely that my father had any thought of ever making them public. They had been neither collected together nor classified in any way. Why then did he write them? Doubtless, we will never know for certain. Probably, he wrote them for himself alone. Those who undergo moving spiritual experiences sometimes write such notes in order to help them remember the nature and intensity of their experience later on, when their memory of the events has grown dim. Whatever the reasons (and it is possible that my father wrote these notes simply in response to an impulse of the moment) they remain for us very precious documents indeed.

The earliest of these notes which we have discovered is dated August 15, 1952, a time when my father was Ambassador in Paris. The note, translated from the French, reveals the very careful organization with which he approached his time of prayer:

> "Today, as usual, I started by thanking God for allowing me to come to see Him. Then, as is my custom, I said I had come to adore Him, Creator of Heaven and Earth. After a minute or two (I think, but am not sure of the time) I said to Him (a) that I wanted to love Him more and more, (b) that I know He loves me, (c) asked Him to show me how to love Him as I did not know and needed His help. I then had a surprise; I began to repeat, in a way which was both intense and spontaneous, that I loved Him, thanking Him for giving me the grace to love Him thus. For some time I *could not* move on to the next point, but kept repeating that I loved Him and wanted to love Him more.
>
> I never passed on to the next point—firstly I was held back at this moment of love and also had no desire to leave it—the next point usually was that I wished to conform my will to His. After this my custom was to ask for graces for certain persons who were suffering or who need God's help for various reasons."

A note dated Sunday, November 23, 1952, reveals by contrast a much more intimate union with Jesus. The wording shows an astonishing ardour and simplicity for a man of 64 to express:

"During the half-hour of prayer I have been asking Jesus for some time now to give me His love with which to love Him, to let me thirst for Him as He thirsts for me, and to hunger for Him as He hungers for me, but I was always a little hesitant. This morning however after Communion I lost my hesitation—I felt that Christ being in me and I in Him, He could increase—and I decrease to such a degree that He *could* in time say over me 'This is my body' and so it seems to me that I in Him might love Him as He loves me, thirst for Him as He thirsts for me, hunger for Him as He hungers for me—And so with confidence I shall say in future 'Christ give me Your love with which to love You, let me thirst for You as You thirst for me, hunger for You as You hunger for me.' Thus shall I be able to love Him as He desires—Any other way is unworthy of His love for me."

A note dated March 11, 1953, undoubtedly written during the course of one of his official visits as Ambassador, shows that on certain particularly privileged occasions, he did not hesitate to exceed the normal time he had allotted for prayer. This note suggests that on the contrary, his period of prayer continued from the time he awoke in the morning through a considerable portion of the day:

"Yesterday morning at Reims I was in a state of prayer for a longer continuous time than ever before. I gave instructions to be wakened at 7 o'clock to attend 8 o'clock Mass. I woke up a little after 6 o'clock and at once began loving affective prayer[9] without any effort and continued until 7 o'clock. During the 8 o'clock Mass in the crypt of the Cathedral same loving affective prayer all the time— After breakfast we returned to the Cathedral for our half-hour's 'oraison'. Once again I felt very near, so near, Jesus and this continued during the visit of the Cathedral until

[9] The term "affective prayer" comes up time and time again in these notes. "This type of prayer is a personal audience or a loving conversation with God, it is capable of as many variations as there are persons. . . . The great thing is to talk to our Lord in one's own words, quite simply, about any topic that is of mutual interest. . . . For some souls, whose minds are filled with the truths therein contained, the Holy Name of Jesus is sufficient prayer." Father Boylan, *Difficulties in Mental Prayer*, p. 31, M. H. Gill & Son, Dublin, 1943.

we got into the car to return to Paris—From 6 o'clock till 11.30 I experienced several touches of sweetness.

I did not write this down last night because I was too tired."

As a family we used to love to go together to Vezelay, a small town in Burgundy where may be found one of the most beautiful romanesque basilicas in France. A friend had set aside a small house for the use and enjoyment of my parents and they were able to pass the occasional holiday there. Thus it was that my father found himself in Vezelay during the Feast of Pentecost in 1953, when he wrote the following note, a note which reveals a remarkable milestone in his spiritual life:

"After breakfast—following 7:30 Mass—I meant to work a little on an address. I went to a room with my papers and closed the door. Without premeditation on my part, I began to invoke the Holy Spirit in a way I have never done before—in personal, direct, frank and loving affective prayer—I am convinced it was the Holy Spirit in a way acting on and in me. In the past my affective prayer has generally speaking been addressed to Jesus who has become a companion. . . . But this morning invoking the Holy Spirit I prayed in an unaccustomed way also to God the Father and to the Holy Trinity as if They—as well as Jesus—were Beings with whom I was establishing a personal relationship. I also prayed fervently to Our Lady—There were many touches of sweetness during this period which lasted about an hour. As it was then 10:15 I went to High Mass in the Basilica, after which I did a half-hour of prayer in church and later about half an hour at home waiting for Pauline who had gone to Pierre-qui-Vire to fetch Michel.

This afternoon I attended Vespers and Benediction. I have felt a very special call to prayer today, without undue fatigue. Deo Gratias, Spiritui Sancto. My mind goes back to the feast of the Assumption last year, Mary's day of glory, marked a turning point in my spiritual life. So I believe does the Holy Spirit's feast mark one today."

My father, as we have seen, on certain privileged occasions, did not limit his period of prayer to a single half-hour. There were times when, apparently in response to a special call from God, he began praying as soon as he woke up; certain of his notes reveal

14

that for him the presence of God remained alive and acute throughout the day. As Robert Speaight[10] so well observed, from all evidence
he was a man who walked with God.

On the 1st of January, 1954, my father retired from External
Affairs. My parents left Paris and, after some months of rest in
Europe, they returned to Canada where they installed themselves
in a small apartment on Sherbrooke Street in Montreal. For my
father, the years of retirement which followed, falling as they did
between his active life in Paris and the beginning of his tour of duty
as Governor General, were particularly painful. His enforced in-
activity weighed heavily upon him. We have few spiritual notes
which date from this period but one of them shows how simple
and uncomplicated his spiritual life became and how deep was his
union with Christ:

> "Yesterday morning I left the apartment at 7. . . . With-
> out any premeditation I began to talk to Jesus as if he were
> by my side just as I would to an old friend. I said how
> pleased I was to be going to Mass with Him. . . This is the
> first time I have been on such easy conversation terms with
> Jesus—without any effort whatever."

If it is true that my father did not read during his periods of
silent prayer, it is nonetheless true that his worship was nourished
by the writings of the Saints, particularly by works on mysticism
and the life of prayer.

Among the mystics, my father gave St. John of the Cross the place
of honour. He would say now and then with a disarming smile and
a touch of mischief: "It is John of the Cross who is my spiritual
director. Not too bad, eh?" Indeed it was the complete works of
John of the Cross, together with those of St. Teresa of Avila which
were constantly at his bedside. How frequently we found him, after
he had taken his breakfast in bed, or late in the evening, pencil in
hand reading and re-reading some passage or other from one of
these two Saints.

My father's attraction to St. John of the Cross came possibly
from the way St. John talked of difficulties in faith. My Father's
spiritual notes may give the impression that he enjoyed some special experiences, but in reality, his life was dominated not so much
by luminous insights as by faith, with all the difficulties it implies.
The following passage, written on April 5, 1953 while he was still
Ambassador in Paris, seems to bear out this conviction:

> "This morning in bed before rising after some affective

[10] *The Tablet*, March 8, 1967.

prayer I found myself asking Jesus to take me by the hand, and lead me through the darkness. . . . During the day I read the remaining seven paragraphs of chapter 16, book 2, of 'The Dark Night of the Soul' and was struck with St. John of the Cross' clear and convincing explanation of the line: 'In darkness and secure'."

The books written by Father Boylan had as we know a great influence on his life, and he returned to them frequently. The first of them which he read, *Difficulties in Mental Prayer* and then later, *This Tremendous Lover*, profoundly marked his spiritual life. He seems to have found in them precisely what he most needed at the time. He liked Father Boylan's style and found in his writings both spiritual sensitivity and sound theology based upon the writings of the Saints. In reading these books, my father began to understand what it meant to love God, an attitude so different to that of fear. Little by little, he began to realize that God seeks the hearts of men and wants earnestly to enter into a loving relationship with them. Through the quotations which Father Boylan used and through the bibliography his books supplied, my father was led to read other spiritual writers; St. Marguerite-Marie Alacoque; Abbé Saudreau on the life of mysticism; Father Paulain, particularly his work entitled *Grâces d'oraison*; St. Louis Marie Grignon de Montfort, particularly the *Traité de la vraie dévotion à la Sainte Vierge*; and many others.

One might also mention the books written by Father Dehau, a prominent French Dominican who, before his death in 1957 had been a friend of Leon Bloy and had greatly influenced the lives of Jacques and Raissa Maritain, Van der Meer de Walcheren and so many others. Although my father had never met Father Dehau, he held him in high regard, as these words translated from a letter written in French on March 6, 1958 bear witness:

"Yes, Father Dehau is an extraordinary person and more than that, he is a Saint. I would say that he will live forever in his books, and for the well-being of many."

During the last six years of his life he read no less than six times the autobiography of St. Teresa of Lisieux, a young French Carmelite nun who died at the age of 24 in 1897. The book he used was a simple paperback edition on the last page of which he inscribed the date on which he finished each reading. It may well be that my father's attraction to the writings of this young and loveable

Saint, writings which radiate confidence and simplicity, reveals much of the nature of his own spirituality.

But it would be wrong to suggest that my father was satisfied simply by a life of prayer. He loved as well to share with others his faith and the strength of prayer and to bear witness to its great importance. In an address which he gave in the Anglican Church of St. Bartholomew in Ottawa on Sunday, November 15, 1964, he declared:

> "There are here, as you observe, several commemorative plaques that recall past tenants of Government House. One feels their presence. Why did they come? To pray—only to pray, but that is everything. If one could only realize the power of prayer!
>
> The Old and the New Testament abound in exhortations to prayer—Christ in St. Luke's Gospel says: 'Keep watch, then, praying at all times, so that you may be found worthy to come safe through all that lies before you, and stand erect to meet the presence of the Son of Man'."
>
> My most fervent hope is that prayer may draw us together. We have so much in common to pray for."

But if he spoke of the importance of prayer, one could not say that he did so in a preaching or dogmatic manner. On the whole, he spoke very little in public about his faith in God. Rather it was by other means, by the warm feeling of good will he seemed to radiate, by his profound and extraordinary appreciation of others, by the serenity of his bearing perhaps—in all these ways he transmitted a sense of the presence of God to others. It was this characteristic which prompted Cardinal Léger in a talk on television to say that "God's presence was his habitual dwelling place."

Father Gay added these words: "All those who came to him were deeply impressed by the atmosphere of peace which surrounded him and of which he was the centre. God Himself flowed out from this man into those around him. Certain men leave behind them an impression of importance; he, a trail of peace and gentleness, and an aura of nobility which was more than human, the nobility of God Himself."

It would, be wrong however to suggest that the time he spent in prayer removed my father from the realities of every day life. We, who knew him, are convinced that far from taking him away from an awareness of his duties to his country, his prayer life formed the foundation of both his moral rectitude and of his sensitivity to others. We must remember that it was the same person who wrote the spiritual notes quoted and who led a life full of responsibilities and activities. Those around him saw only his meticulous dedication to his work and felt the radiance of his goodness, but the secret source of both these qualities was unknown to them.

"The weakness of human means is a source of strength"[10]

In his inaugural speech as Governor General, on September 15, 1959, my father said: "My first words are a prayer. May Almighty God, in His infinite wisdom and mercy bless the sacred mission which has been entrusted to me by Her Majesty the Queen and help me to fulfill it in all humility. In exchange for His strength, I offer my weakness. May He give peace to this beloved land of ours and to those who live in it the grace of mutual understanding."

The profound link between his own weakness and God's strength and mercy was one of the foundation stones of his spiritual life, as is shown by so many of his letters, particularly this one which he wrote to a Carmelite nun, a friend of my mother. The letter is dated 22nd August 1959 just prior to his installation as Governor General, and is here translated from the French.

"To know that you keep me in your heart and prayers is so necessary for me; for without the prayers of those who love me in the Heart of Jesus I would be panic stricken, and I would not dare at my age to undertake the responsibilities that await me.

Knowing that I lack the necessary strength, I can only hope that my very weakness will save me. I say therefore to Jesus, 'I place my heart in Yours. Do with it what You will. May it beat in tune with Your own heart if that should be Your wish, but if not, may it be consumed in the fire of Your love.' Jesus exchanged hearts with Saint Margaret Mary and with other Saints. Pray that He may grant me also this grace, without which I will never be able to accomplish the mission which has been confided to my wife and to myself. Ask Him to give me strength, His strength, from day to day, sufficient unto each day. Until now He seems to bestow his grace upon me in this

[10] Words of Charles de Foucauld underlined by my father in *Itinéraire Spirituel de Charles de Foucauld*, Edition du Seuil, 1958, p. 252. English translation: *Spiritual Autobiography of Charles de Foucauld*, P. J. Kennedy & Sons, New York.

18

way—just enough to meet the needs of each day. I often have the impression, and I hope I am not being presumptuous in thinking so, that He keeps me as it were on a leash. There are times when I feel very strong and sure of myself, especially in public, and this is important in front of others. But there are other moments which those around me do not know of, when I am overwhelmed with a feeling of utter weakness and impotence. In these moments of weakness when Jesus pulls upon the leash as it were, to remind me of my nothingness, I say to Him 'Jesus I abandon myself to Your Merciful Love' but I do not always say it with complete and utter confidence. Pray then, my beloved friend, that Jesus will give me the grace to believe, that He will give me total faith, that He will never forsake me. I am, as it were, like St. Peter trying to walk on the surface of the water. . . .

I have spoken enough of myself. To conclude I can say only 'May His Will be done.' My tour of duty as Governor General is to be of five year's duration. It will be for Jesus to decide how long I will be able in weakness to serve Him and to serve my country."

In another letter dated August 26, 1960, he wrote, "I try to give myself up completely to Divine Providence. I feel that only in weakness can I glorify God. Often exhaustion overwhelms me."

By giving him strength in these moments of fatigue, and by giving him light and guidance when he needed them, my father felt, that God was providing proof of His wondrous loving-kindness, and of the love of the Holy Spirit. His weakness and his infirmities, from which he could never escape, helped him to become really humble in face of the responsibilities and the honours thrust upon him, and to appreciate to the full, the possibilities for good which still lay open to him.

During his radio and television message broadcast on his first New Year's Day as Governor General, he declared to the Canadian people:

"I have one request to make of you. Whatever your religion may be, pray that, in the coming year, God give me a humble and contrite heart."

No one was more aware than my father himself of his own physical, intellectual, and spiritual limitations; indeed, so conscious was he of them that it always came as a source of astonishment to him to discover that all his shortcomings in no way prevented him from becoming an instrument of God's grace. He spoke often and with great admiration of those religious men and women who in their generosity achieved great acts of renunciation and faith. But he did so always in a way which suggested that he felt that their accomplishments were completely beyond his own abilities, and that he himself would be incapable of imitating their example.

"I am reading the life of St. John of the Cross to your mother, he wrote to one of us on September 23, 1957. What a man! I could never hope to follow his example, having neither the strength nor the courage, but at least he inspires me with a feeling of humility. This especially, I think, is what I gain from the lives of the Saints. How small one feels compared to them."

He underlined the following passage in one of Father Boylan's books, and I am certain that he always tried to remain faithful to the ideas it expresses:

"True humility is always accompanied by boundless confidence. Pride sees in our own self with its apparent excellence, our claim on God's co-operation, and on God's rewards; but even pride must admit that the very basis of such a claim sets a limit to it. Humility bases its confidence on personal poverty of spirit, and on the infinite mercy of God; it takes its stand on the merits of Christ, knowing that then nothing will be wanting to us in any grace."[11]

In no way did he let the honours which people piled upon him go to his head. It was accurately said of him that he accepted them in spite of himself; certainly they left him not a whit less sensitive to the needs and suffering of others. In his heart of hearts he considered himself no more than a lowly servant of God, as the signature of one of his letters bears witness, "The humble servant of Christ the King".

A passage in the very moving sermon given by the Reverend John Gladstone at Yorkminster Park Baptist Church, Toronto on March 30, 1967, admirably summarizes this aspect of his character:

"We can say, in conclusion, that his goodness found expression in *a humble walk with God*. Indeed, this was the secret of all that he was and did. When he used the word 'God', it was in no sense a glib, meaningless catch-

[11] *The Spiritual Life of the Priest*, p. 108.

word. It was the outward sign of an inward conviction, the natural language of someone to whom the habit of prayer was a daily discipline. His God was alive and active, a God to be worshipped and served, a God to whom in the end a man must give an account of his stewardship. 'My first words are a prayer . . .'—so began the short speech he made when he was sworn in as Governor General. 'If we believe the Lord is our strength,' he said on another occasion, 'then why not act as if it is true?' So General Vanier believed and lived. He could walk in high places with a sure and steady tread because he was accustomed in all places to walk humbly with God. He had the inner strength and invincible serenity that are ever God's gifts to those who wait upon Him, and draw deeply on His inexhaustible resources."

To conclude these few paragraphs on his humility, I'd like to quote from a letter which he wrote on August 20, 1961 to a friend of my mother's and where he speaks of her with such kind simplicity.

"You can't imagine to what extent I need your prayers. I feel so clearly that in my great weakness, it is the prayer of my friends which sustains me.

Pauline is admirable. Not only does she second me, but she surpasses me in our tasks and duties. She is the best half of the team and with her failing eyesight which makes her suffer, that demands great courage."

"Unless you become like little children you shall not enter the Kingdom of Heaven"[12]

If my father prayed as he did, it was because he really believed in the message of the gospels. Jesus and His Holy Spirit were to him realities. He believed that the Spirit lived and that he could be united to Him. He had an instinctive horror of the complicated and of theological discussions. Among his favourite passages in the New Testament and which he underlined were those in which Christ pointed out that if one's faith is the size even of a mustard seed one will be able to move mountains. "Have faith in God," says Jesus. "I tell you solemnly if anyone says to this mountain get up

12 Matthew, 18:3.

and throw yourself into the sea with no hesitation in his heart, but believing that what he says will happen, it will be done for him. I tell you therefore everything you ask and pray for, believe that you have it already and it will be yours."[13]

He was particularly fond of the story of the man who had been blind from birth and was healed by Jesus. The leaders of the synagogue attempted to make the man concede that Christ must be in league with the devil to have such a gift. Whereupon the blind man replied with the utmost simplicity, "Whether sinner or not I do not know, all I know is that once I was blind and now I can see." (John 9:25.) My father was deeply struck by the common sense aspect of this last remark.

His faith was equally simple. Before he gained it, he was blind. Now that he had it, he could see. Without faith, nothing made sense to him. It was as simple as that. It was hardly surprising that he felt no need for theological propositions. With youthful pretentions, I would sometimes put to him some new theological thoughts. "That must be very interesting," he would say and add with a mischievous twinkle, "perhaps you should tell it to your mother." So direct was his own faith—diamond-like, said Cardinal Leger[14]—that he felt no need to be clouded with unspiritual considerations or fine points of doctrine or dogma. So complete was it that no contentious evidence or sad calamities could shake it. "We cannot know the meaning of innocent suffering or calamity," he would say, "but we know that God is love and therefore all these things which happen must happen for some purpose and in the end all will work out for the best."

He loved the passage (Luke 10, 21) where Jesus says, "I bless you Father for hiding these things from the cunning and the clever and revealing them to mere children."[15] His desire to become like a child is manifested in a moving way in this letter to a Carmelite sister dated 6th February 1959:

"When you pray for me will you pray especially that the Blessed Virgin ask Her Son to give me the heart of a child. I know that this is much to ask but I would ask it nonetheless because otherwise Jesus would not be pleased with

13 Mark, 23:24.
14 "Those who had the privilege of knowing intimately Georges Vanier, discovered quickly the place that God holds in the life of a real believer. His soul was never troubled by doubt and his diamond-like faith which guided his life was the main motivation of all his actions." Cardinal Léger, Sermon during the Funeral Mass, Basilica, Ottawa, March 8, 1967.
15 Luke, 10, 21.

me and I do not wish to displease Him. I am sure that He will answer your prayer. You love Him and He has no defence against love. Dom Lefebvre[16] says that God does not belong to Himself, what a consoling thought. He is at the mercy of our love: let us then launch the assault. But this ardent desire to have the heart of a child can only come from Jesus and the little Thérèse of Lisieux teaches that if Jesus gives such desire then it can be fulfilled."[17]

"Fiat Voluntas Dei"

In a spiritual note dated the 25th of February, 1959, written at Montreal before his nomination as Governor General, and at a moment when he seemed to be suffering from extreme exhaustion, my father wrote:

"Morning—very depressed, suffering greatly. 'I can't go on any longer, my God, but may your will be done.' Asking neither to go on suffering nor to die, but showing nonetheless a preference for complete union with God before much longer, giving voice to the hope that my will be similar to His."

This note, as does the brief message sent to one of us just before his last operation:

"All is well. Fiat Voluntas Dei.
Daddy
November 4th, 1966."

shows his complete self-abandonment to the will of God. On another piece of paper, which we found among his belongings after his death, were inscribed the words uttered by Christ on the cross, "Father, into Thy hands I commend my spirit."

Fiat Voluntas Dei! May God's Will be Done. This was the motto he chose to put on his official coat-of-arms when he became Governor General. Thus did he render public and even official that deep motivation of his life, the desire to conform his life and actions to the Will of God. *Fiat* became thus the leitmotiv of many of his

16 Dom Lefebvre, a Benedictine monk, author of a number of spiritual books.
17 Cf. *Autobiography of a Saint, Therese of Lisieux*, translated by Ronald Knox. Collins, London, 1958, p. 194.

decisions. To his doctors as to his friends and family when talking about his health and the possibilities of his remaining or not in office during the last years of his life, he would repeat, "We will wait and see. Fiat Voluntas Dei. It is all in His Hands; if He wants me to stay on He will give me the strength."

"Nothing official yet about my new appointment," he wrote on July 10, 1959, just before his nomination as Governor General, "but it will carry a very heavy burden of responsibility. We will rely entirely on the loving kindness of the Holy Spirit. Everything is in the hands of Jesus. May His will be done.

I have not asked my doctor whether my health will permit taking on such responsibilities. I do not want to make my acceptance subject to a medical certificate. But I have simply said to Jesus, 'I sincerely believe that it is my duty to accept. I know that you will give me the strength I need if it is your wish that I perform the mission which has been entrusted to me. If the opposite is true, that is if your wish should be that I do not accept this post, then you will not support me. Whichever shall be your will, I accept in advance.' In this way everything is simple and straightforward, I have no worry whatsoever, and I merely put myself in the hands of the Lord'."

"It is obvious," he wrote to me a few weeks later, on October 16, 1959, after his installation as Governor General, "it is more and more obvious that God is sustaining me. Left to my own human resources, I could never accomplish all that I am undertaking at this moment. I sense very clearly and irrefutably that the prayer which I made at my installation is being answered, that He is exchanging His strength for my weakness. But for how long? May His will be done. Please continue to pray for me. . ."

"With regard to the future, I abandon myself to Divine Providence," he wrote to a friend on August 31, 1963. "I say to Jesus, 'if you still want to use me, lend me your heart—mine alone can do nothing—you can substitute yours for mine if you so wish. It is an exchange which you made with others—if on the contrary, you feel that I should go, may your will be done.' Pray that I may be sincere with myself when I speak thus. It is so easy to make wonderful phrases, hoping that the will of Jesus is the same as our own. Anyway, we will soon see what are His plans. We will be back again into full activity in September next."

On his bedside table he kept a copy he had made of a passage from Father de Caussade's book, *Abandonment to Divine Providence*:

"And souls who are truly abandoned to God's will are not preoccupied by their infirmities, except in the case of obvious illnesses which by their very nature oblige them to take to their beds and submit to appropriate treatment. The feelings of listlessness and helplessness experienced by such souls are but illusion and semblance, to be braved with confidence. God sends them and allows them so that the soul may exercise faith and abandonment which is the real remedy. Without giving so much as a thought to such feelings they must generously continue on their way, doing God's work and bearing the suffering He sends, making use of their bodies without hesitation, as one makes use of a hired horse, destined to perish after serving all and sundry. This is better than any amount of coddling which only impairs the strength of the spirit. This spiritual vigour has an extraordinary power of sustaining a weak body, and one year of such a noble and generous life is worth more than centuries of care and anxiety."[18]

With increasing age and his infirmity, he tended to worry about his health. He took his own pulse frequently, and was absolutely meticulous in taking the various medicines prescribed by his physicians. And yet he spoke so often of the importance of abandoning oneself to God—is there a contradiction between these two attitudes? Or does the second indicate a struggle to overcome the first? Putting himself in the hands of God did not mean for him neglecting his health. He did everything he could to take care of himself simply so that he might better be able to serve. But in other ways his self-abandonment was very real: certainly he took no concern whatever for his own future. He genuinely left everything in the hands of God.

This confidence in Divine aid, and his wish to have his own will conform to God's, sometimes complicated life for us all. His natural temperament was to put off making decisions, "sufficient unto the day being the evils thereof". His spiritual life and his complete confidence in God reinforced this natural tendency. But often it seemed to us that he sometimes put off making decisions about relatively minor things.

"During the coming year," he wrote on December 15, 1958,

18 *L'Abandon à la Divine Providence*, Gabalda and Cie, 1934, Paris, Vol. I, p. 132.

when he and my mother were living in a small apartment in Mont-real, "we really must consider the question of where we're going to live. But for the moment I shall give no thought to it. I will leave everything in God's hands and I have told Him so. In all probability signs will be given us when the time comes to make a decision."

We can all remember how difficult it was for him to reach a decision even on so elementary a question as to where and when we should take our family summer vacation. His hesitation would persist until the point where it was well-nigh impossible to find accommodation. And yet for all that, things had a way of working out in the end.

These times of unjustified procrastination tended to blind us to the wisdom of his caution on so many other occasions. It is true that he was extremely reluctant to risk making a wrong decision, but his primary motivation was simply to try first to find out what God's will might be. He believed that the Lord would show his preference by exterior providential signs, if only one knew enough to wait for them. And how often did such waiting prove the better part of wisdom!

And remarkably enough, while this trust in Divine guidance often promoted a sense of great caution, at the same time his profound sense of duty often made him genuinely daring. Every major event in his life, his recovery after the grievous wounds he suffered during the First World War, and the many careers he followed, all gave him the distinct impression of a Divinity shaping his end. With this impression it was not unnatural that he interpreted his appointment as Governor General as another step, albeit a crowning one, in a life that had been ordered from its beginning. Often when he recalled his services as aide-de-camp to two Governors General, Lord Byng and Lord Willingdon, between 1925 and 1928, and how these services prepared him for his own tour of duty as Governor General, he would say with a certain amazement, "One would really think that it had all been planned." His years spent in the army, and his service as a diplomat in London and Paris, took on the appearance of a succession of preparations for his final appointment. It was thus as Governor General, more than ever before, that he felt that he had the opportunity to become a real channel of God's providence, and his sole desire was to acknowledge this Divine grace and fulfill the mission confided to him.

"Striving"

"Striving, striving, and more striving—every day, every hour, every moment. . . I am bold enough to say, though not in the literal sense, that I almost prefer striving without success to success without striving."

These remarks, made by my father at the College of St. Jean de Breboeuf at Montreal on November 1, 1960, echo words of Charles de Foucauld which my father had underlined:

> "Indeed, if the efforts one makes for the salvation of souls remain unsuccessful for the latter, they are the more fruitful for the one who makes them. For unsuccess makes him more like Jesus, listened to by so few, followed by so few, despised, scorned and jeered at during His lifetime."[19]

When my father spoke of his feeling of weakness—and sometimes he would say to us: "Really, I feel devoid of strength, utterly useless"—it was no exaggeration, but a constant physical reality. He was called upon to make continuing and unrelenting effort. The various spiritual notes which we include in this volume may perhaps give the impression that his spiritual life was spontaneous and easy. If he noted the rather special graces of peace and love which he experienced was it not that these appeared to him as exceptional in his life which was normally marked by effort and faith.

There can be no question that to preserve his faith my father was called upon to show extraordinary courage and preseverance in meeting the obstacles placed in his way. It seems likely that he accepted the need to struggle with these obstacles with great simplicity, saying to himself that though he could not understand the reason for them, it was his duty to accept them. During the last few weeks of his life he spoke often with my mother of faith, its significance and its expression. Was it not for this reason that he so loved to read and re-read St. Teresa of Lisieux, who herself had had so many challenges to her faith. Undoubtedly, he found fresh inspiration and encouragement in her writings.

But it was on the physical plane that his efforts were most obvious. The high amputation of his leg, a result of wartime injury, meant frequent pain and almost continual discomfort. Particularly during the later years of his life, walking even short distances, and

[19] *Spiritual Autobiography of Charles de Foucauld*, J.-F. Six, P. J. Kennedy & Sons, New York, 1958, p. 34.

for that matter merely standing, sapped what little strength he had to the point of exhaustion. During the last weeks all at Government House noticed his heroic efforts to comply with his doctor's recommendations that he come down from his room as often as possible and take as great a part as he could in the life of the house, the better to promote his recovery from a surgical operation the preceding autumn. He hoped so much to be able to continue to serve his country during its centennial year, feeling that Canada would have a special need for someone of French descent at such a time. But the effort required was simply too much for him.

All his life long he showed himself to be a man endowed with exceptional courage. The same bravery which he had shown on the battlefield, where it had won him recognition and so many awards, was no less needed in everyday life to accept the handicaps he suffered, to make the efforts required in remaining faithful to his sense of duty, and finally in keeping him always and simply master of himself. In a letter of condolence written at the time of his death, a mother of four who was herself blind and had lost a leg, declared that his courage was for her "a beacon in the face of adversity".

And yet he would frequently say to us that he must be careful not to indulge in what he called "the sins of old age": constant complaining and querulousness. "If ever," he told us, "you catch me bemoaning my aches and pains, you must remind me at once of what I am doing and I shall stop immediately." We never had to remind him for we never heard him complain. Certainly no one can accuse him of "the sins of old age", for far from being querulous, his mind seemed almost always composed and serene, and his heart young and gay; the rare moments when he lost his temper were all but lost in his much more usual mood of relaxed good humour.

He showed astonishing self-control, and this in turn required great effort on his part. In many ways, by temperament, he had all the volatility of his French and Irish ancestors. His instincts were to become angry or exasperated easily, but very rarely did he allow such reactions to be visible externally. And on the very few occasions when he did show even so much as a gesture of impatience he would profoundly and sincerely apologize afterwards.

Some time before his death he agreed that a television team might come and take some shots inside Rideau Hall. Thus it was that the director of the team telephoned one morning to see which day would be convenient. Since the Governor General was plan-

His Excellency's personal coat of arms and
motto "God's Will Be Done". (See page 23)

With daughter, Thérèse, at Vezelay, France 1959

At prayer in the Quebec Basilica

Mme. Vanier, Pope John XXIII, General Vanier, and the author

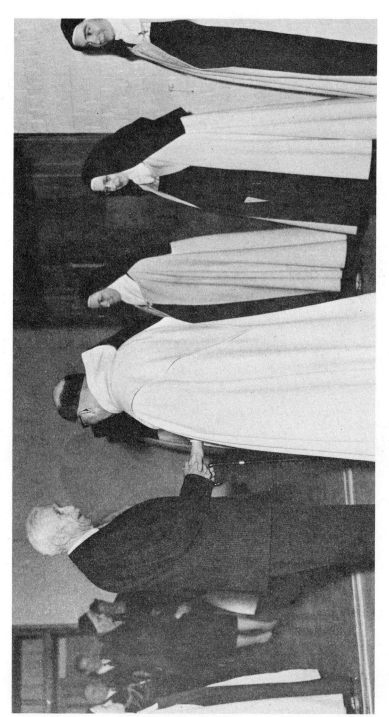

His Excellency visits the Montreal Carmel 1962

Facing: At His Excellency's installation as Governor-General of Canada, Ottawa, September 15th, 1959. Behind on His Excellency's right is the Rt. Hon. John G. Diefenbaker, Prime Minister of Canada

Below: Reading the speech from the throne, Ottawa, April 5, 1965. Seated on His Excellency's right is the Rt. Hon. Lester B. Pearson, Prime Minister of Canada

Their Excellencies with their grandchildren in Government House, Ottawa. This photograph was Their Excellencies' Christmas Card in 1966

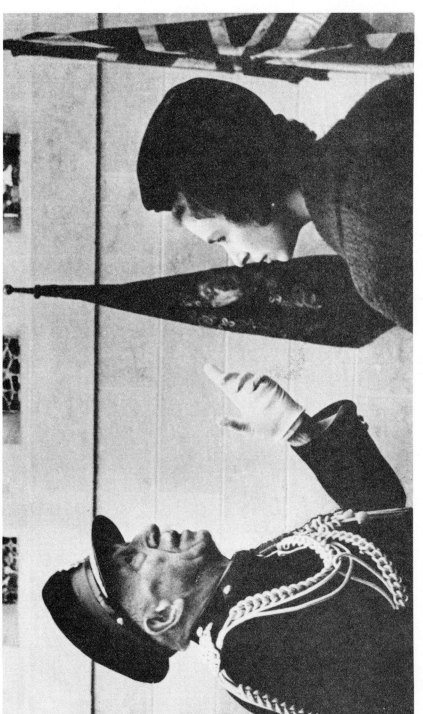

With Her Majesty the Queen at the dedication of the Royal 22nd Regiment's Memorial in the Citadel, Quebec City, October 10, 1964

The Chapel in Government House during His Excellency's term of office

Acte d'offrande

propre *Justice*, et recevoir de votre *Amour* la possession
éternelle de *Vous-même*. Je ne veux point d'autre *Trône*
et d'autre *Couronne* que *Vous*, ô mon *Bien Aimé* !...

A vos yeux le temps n'est rien, un seul jour est comme
mille ans, vous pouvez donc en un instant me préparer
à paraître devant vous...

Afin de vivre dans un acte de parfait Amour, JE
M'OFFRE COMME VICTIME D'HOLOCAUSTE A VOTRE
AMOUR MISÉRICORDIEUX, vous suppliant de
me consumer sans cesse, laissant déborder en mon âme
les flots de *tendresse infinie* qui sont renfermés en vous
et qu'ainsi je devienne *Martyre* de votre *Amour*, ô
mon Dieu !...

Que ce *Martyre* après m'avoir préparée à paraître
devant vous me fasse enfin mourir et que mon âme
s'élance sans retard dans l'éternel embrassement de
Votre Miséricordieux Amour...

Je veux, ô mon *Bien Aimé*, à chaque battement de
mon cœur vous renouveler cette offrande un nombre
infini de fois jusqu'à ce que les ombres s'étant évanouies,
je puisse vous redire mon *Amour* dans un *Face à Face*
Éternel !...

Marie, Françoise, Thérèse de l'Enfant-Jésus
et de la Sainte Face rel. carm. ind.

Fête de la Très Sainte Trinité.
Le 9 Juin de l'an de grâce 1895 [1].

1. Il existe dans les Archives du Carmel de Lisieux une première
version de cet Acte d'Offrande, rédigée de la main de Sainte Thérèse
de l'Enfant-Jésus. Ce texte a été reproduit en fac-similé dans la grande
édition des *Manuscrits Autobiographiques*. Il comporte quelques légères
divergences avec la version définitive que nous donnons ici. Celle-ci
a été rédigée par Thérèse pour Mère Agnès de Jésus, largement diffu-
sée dans la suite et approuvée par l'Église.

The Lying-In-State in the Ballroom of Government House, Ottawa, March 1967

ning to receive the Prime Minister in the course of the afternoon, permission was given to the television crew to film the event in my father's study. Thinking that such a filming required no more than one or two persons with a small portable camera, my father was hardly prepared when he arrived for the rendezvous to find his dearly loved study in complete disorder, furniture pushed into corners, huge pieces of equipment dominating the room, and lights and wires in all direction. Highly annoyed, he indignantly ordered that everything be removed at once. The several members of the team, in embarrassed consternation, set about removing the equipment as quickly as they could. Esmond Butler, Secretary to the Governor General, came at once to try to act as intermediary. It soon became evident that my father was already regretting his loss of temper. After a moment's discussion it was agreed that the team should reinstall its equipment. My father withdrew, and when he returned shortly after for his meeting with the Prime Minister he began by making fun of himself for his previous impetuosity. He allowed an extravagant amount of time for the photographers to take their pictures, and afterwards made a point of shaking the hand of each member of the crew and of apologizing most sincerely to their director.

Happily the mastery which he usually showed of his emotions in no way made him cold or imperturbable or stripped him of his natural spontaneity. His sense of humour, his love of the ridiculous, and his irrepressible vivacity prevented him from appearing stoic. He could tell stories that the most staid listener found it impossible not to laugh at, and he always had the right tale, appropriately droll for each occasion. Often he would recount the most ludicrous stories with an air of utmost seriousness, which of course added to their hilarity, and often took the earnest listener by amazed surprise.

He would tell a gathering which he felt had grown overly serious how, for example, he had that morning invited his infant grandchildren to come to his room to play with razor blades; he would then watch with a straight face their reactions of dismay and astonishment.

He could even make fun of the source of so much of his pain and exhaustion, his amputated leg. A friend remonstrated with him when he accepted the post of Governor General at the advanced age of 72: "Why, good Heavens," the friend expostulated, "you've already got one foot in the grave!" "True," my father returned, "but after all it's been there for 42 years!"

29

It would never occur to him to dramatize his handicap in order to solicit sympathy: the exact opposite was the case, for he loved to joke about his artificial limb. When we were very young children he used to sit us on his knee and say, "Now you will see what a fine Stoic I am" and give us a pin which he would urge us to stick into his leg. Often when we were out walking together he would give his artificial leg a tremendous crack with his cane, and declare to our admiring gaze, "Just see how tough my legs are!"

In remarks which he made at the 28th National Congress of the War Amputees of Canada on October 16, 1961, he included the following unsuspected vignette of history:

> "I thought you might be interested to hear that I have lately been reading a book entitled *One Leg* (unfortunately I can't claim to be its author). It deals with the life of Lord Anglesey, who was a Field-Marshal and commanded the cavalry at the famous battle of Waterloo, where he had the misfortune to lose a leg to one of the last shots fired. I should say, perhaps, *good* fortune, because three weeks after losing his leg the Prince Regent made Lord Oxbridge a Marquis. I am not at all sure that the Prince Regent would have done so if Lord Oxbridge hadn't lost a leg, I am not sure I'd be here if I hadn't lost mine."[20]

Perhaps the story which best illustrates my father's ability to make light of his own handicap was one which he loved to tell—how, in spite of the loss of a leg, he applied for a position in a regular army regiment:

> ". . . My legal life was rather sedentary, and I seemed to be losing weight at a rather alarming rate. Therefore, when the Royal Vingt-Deuxieme Regiment was being re-formed, I decided to return to the Army. So I went to Ottawa, where Sir Arthur Currie was then Inspector General of the forces—a post that no longer exists, in case anybody should think that I am inventing something that did not then exist—and I told him—no, I didn't *tell* him anything, but I asked whether he could find a place for me in the Regiment. He laughed at me—nicely, but he laughed. He said, 'You have lost a leg'; so I said, 'I know that, but don't you want a few officers with brains as well as legs?' What he really liked, I think, was my modesty!

[20] Talk delivered at the 28th National Congress of the War Amputees of Canada, October 16, 1961.

I left him without any expectations at all. We both laughed and we both knew, or I felt anyway, that there was no hope; but within three weeks I was appointed Second in Command."

"My son, when the Lord corrects you do not treat it lightly," my father underlined in the 12th chapter of St. Paul's letter to the Hebrews, "but do not get discouraged when he reprimands you. Suffering is part of your training. God is treating you as his sons. . . . Of course punishment is most painful at the time and far from pleasant but later in those on whom it has been used, it bears fruit in peace and greatness." These words seem to have had a special meaning for him, as perhaps more particularly did the passage which follows: "So hold up your limp arms and steady your trembling knees and smooth out the path you tread; then injured limb will not be wrenched, it will grow strong again."[21] My father underlined similar passages in St. Matthew's gospel:

"Anyone who does not take up his cross . . . is not worthy of me"[22]

". . . but my yoke is easy and my burden light."[23]

Whether he was tempted to compare his own physical condition to St. Paul's "thorn in the flesh", we do not know, but it was certain that his infirmity enhanced, rather than diminished his faith.

"Behold thy Mother"[24]

My father had a deep respect and affection for those whom he felt were close to God. As was said already, this deep admiration was the fruit of his own real humility. He himself felt spiritually and physically incapable of emulating their example. He admired in them what he seemingly would have liked to have done himself and in contacts with them, he felt to a certain extent a divine influence.

Christian tradition springing from the Prophets Hosaiah, Isaiah, and Ezekiel, has always affirmed that God wishes to establish with man relations that are comparable to those existing in marriage.

[21] St. Paul's Epistle to the Hebrews, 12, 5-7, and 11-12.
[22] Matthew 10:38.
[23] Matthew 11:30.
[24] John, 19:27.

"Your creator is your spouse," announced Isaiah.[25] Christian mystical tradition, of which some of the greatest exponents are Saint Bernard, Saint Teresa of Avila and Saint John of the Cross, took the inspired writing of "The Songs of Songs" as the immediate figure of the love that unites the soul to God. Thus it is that those who consecrate themselves to Jesus totally, desiring only to follow Him, have always been known as spouses of Christ. This tradition helps us to understand references such as those in the following extract from a letter that my father wrote to a Carmelite Sister on 24th January 1961:

> "Your letter deeply touched me, and I must admit even to tears. You see I have such a love for the spouses of Jesus that I cannot come near them—even in thought—without receiving a wonderful grace. And when the heart is linked to this grace—the Heart of Jesus, your heart and those of your Carmelite Sisters, and mine—it appears as a special benediction which is almost a sign for me of divine predilection. May God render to you a hundredfold the good you have done to me. . . ."

We have here the secret of his love for the Virgin Mary. With his deep faith, he believed in the possibility of communing with those who were already in God and with God in the Heavenly Kingdom. Just as he had felt a divine grace in knowing certain souls whom he felt were close to God, so he felt a grace in approaching lovingly and in faith the Virgin Mary. Hadn't she lived closer than any to Jesus? And when the apostles had fled did she not remain standing at the foot of the Cross?

My father felt that by approaching Mary lovingly, he would be sanctified, that she would bless him, that she would help him love Jesus and become humble with the heart of a child.

In a spiritual note dated the 29th of January, 1953, my father wrote the following lines, which show clearly the filial confidence which he placed in the Mother of Christ:

> "This morning at the rue Cortambert Chapel, prayer was difficult. In spite of many and fervent appeals to Christ's love there was no feeling in me of response from the Beloved. I then turned to Our Blessed Lady and said something like this—'Please ask Thy Son to grant me the grace to love Him more and more—Do remind Him that

[25] Isaiah, 54:5.

He said to Margaret Mary 'I thirst, I burn with the *desire*: to be loved.' Well, I am here, I am a sinner but I want only to love him—I want to thirst and burn with the *desire* to love Him—but not only the desire: I want to burn with love for Him; If Thy Son wishes He can give me this love, please ask Him.' This was said only a very few minutes before the end of the half hour which had been arid. Suddenly I felt a very sweet touch which warmed my whole being and stirred me to feelings of deep and moving gratitude to the Beloved and to His Mother."

He frequently went to Lourdes, a pilgrimage centre dedicated to the Virgin Mary. He had been for many years deeply impressed by the book *Voyage à Lourdes* by Alexis Carrel, and he had bought many copies and had distributed them to friends. Every time he happened to be near the Pyrenees, he would go there and at least once I remember accompanying him on a pilgrimage he made especially from Paris.

Nor did he ever visit Lourdes without repeating the act of faith made by so many before him: ever since the Virgin Mary appeared to Bernadette at Lourdes in 1858, the sick and physically handicapped had plunged themselves in the icy waters of the springs. My father, who walked with the famous and the mighty, considered it a special privilege to be able to bathe in these waters with the poor, the ill and the deformed.

The letter which follows, written on August 20, 1961, gives us some idea of the impression Lourdes made upon him:

"I know of nothing more moving than the faith of all the sick here—of whom few are healed humanly and physically—but who all leave with the same faith, smiling faces, and the same desire to return. They are all touched deeply by grace, and marked as it were by its seal. They remain the best answer to those who do not understand the spiritual value of suffering and who revolt against it.

My visit to Lourdes is an act of faith, in recognition and thanks for all the supernatural help that has been given me since I am Governor General.

The promise of your prayers deeply touches me. I am so in need of them, I have the certainty that abandoned to my weakness, which is so great, I could not accomplish my mission. I count upon you and the Carmelite Sisters to help me, and I ask Our Lady to thank them for me by drawing down many graces upon them."

Another letter written to a friend, dated 23rd August, 1958, strikes the same note:

"I am praying very particularly to the Blessed Virgin, our beloved Mother, to take you in Her keeping. She will ask Jesus to place you in His heart and there give you protection and strength and grace.

Have no fear, He will sustain you—*just have faith that He will*, nothing else is necessary, only *faith*, that's what Lourdes is, that's its great miracle. Hundreds of thousands come each year, *are not cured* (at least in a physical sense), but leave Lourdes, at peace and serene, without even apparent disappointment and they come back. Every-one of them is a *spiritual* miracle. If there were more obvious miracles, there would be less faith. We must live in faith, says St. John of the Cross. That is the way to saintliness."

It was my father's confidence in the protection of the Virgin Mary that prompted him to place a small tree in the upperhalf of his official coat-of-arms. Many asked him the reason for including this tree. He would explain the other symbols—the steeple of Honfleur, the French seaport, from where his forefathers had sailed for Canada, and the Citadel of Quebec to which he was so deeply attached. He explained the motto on the coat-of-arms "Fiat Voluntas Dei"—"God's Will be done". But he would remain silent concerning the significance of the tree. It was in fact the symbol of Fatima, an important pilgrimage centre in Portugal also dedicated to the Virgin, where in 1917 Mary had appeared standing above a small holm-oak, to three young children. Thus, in his official coat-of-arms, he enshrined his love for the Virgin.

Conscious as he was of his heavy responsibility to God and to his country, my father cherished the opportunity to pray especially for Canada and for Canadians and to ask God's blessing upon them. He recited every year a special prayer that he had had written (of which we give a few extracts) addressed to our Lady since he believed so much in her intercession.

"O my Sovereign Lady, I pray you, lead all Canadians towards the only true happiness, that of seeing and lov-ing your Son, Jesus, for all eternity, Jesus the Word Incarnate, One with God the Father and the Holy Spirit. . . .

Keep us in that true peace which comes from a right relationship between our souls and God and amongst all men. Light the flame of divine love within our hearts . . . let the bonds of brotherly love grow within them. . . . Lead our hearts towards the only truth, preserve them from all error, and in particular keep them from materialism, the materialism that plunges intelligence into darkness and hides the natural law which is the reflection of divine and eternal law. . . .

O Mary, keep watch over all Canadians . . . whatever may be their sins, their religion, or their race. . . . Unite us all more and more to the Heart of your Son, our Brother. Help those who suffer morally and physically. Show your motherly loving-kindness to the humble, to prisoners, and to the poor. Preserve and strengthen our Canadian families, cradles of religion and moral life. Above all protect our young people, growing up as they are in a world in chaos, and needing your Motherly help to resist the many and seductive temptations which surround them."

"Beloved ones let us love one another, as love is from God, and he who loves is born of God and knows God"[26]

It is not always easy for children to speak of their father's love, or to give examples which bring their thoughts and memories to life. There is almost too much to say about the infinite number of ways in which my father showed his love for my mother and each one of us, and to try to do so would be to tresspass in a domain which is almost too private and too personal to be made public. . . . Either that, or we could limit ourselves and give only the most trite and banal examples, and not mention those which we really cherish in our hearts.

For these reasons, in the pages that follow, I will draw on a number of testimonies from others, testimonies expressed at the time of his death, which may give us an inkling of my father's love and generosity.

We were especially touched by the kind words which Catherine

[26] I Epis. St. John 4:7.

Doherty wrote, embodying as they did the feeling that many share, namely that at Rideau Hall they had lost a friend:

"During all of the time of his residency in Government House, he brought to me, and I'm sure to many, comfort. I didn't feel alone when he was there, and again, in some intangible way, I knew that if I needed him for myself or for others, he would give me the greatest gift one person can give to another, the gift of attentiveness, the gift of being a listener, of truly being approachable to any person's need. Somehow, I also knew that even if this particular need of mine whatever it might have been, could not be satisfied, I would be comforted by having explained it to him. It would be his person, his ways, his gently gracious ways, in a word, his love of God and men, that would bring me that comfort."[27]

How beautifully as well did Hugh Kemp express this thought during the radio broadcast of the Governor General's funeral:

". . . He loved us—openly,
And we loved back,
And that fact alone has warmed us
for a century to come.
He has inspired us
to unashamedly love ourselves.
Pray God—so let it be
not only in these days of mourning
but always and forever."

The Anglican Archdeacon of Quebec, Guy Marsten, summarized these thoughts during the funeral service at the Basilica in Quebec:

". . . and in love, that greatest of all Christian virtues, Governor General Vanier was not wanting. His life was couched in love. He loved and cared for his family and we Canadians saw this. He loved and served his Church and we Canadians saw this. He loved and served to the uttermost his Country and we Canadians saw this. He loved us, ourselves, and especially our children, and we knew this and loved him for it. And all this was possible because above all he loved God, and that love permeated and conditioned all his way."

[27] *Restoration*, Combere, Ontario, April 1967.

36

I think it would be fair to say that in fulfilling his rôle as Governor General my father experienced a genuine transformation. During the years when he was Ambassador in Paris, his spiritual life had begun to deepen. The spiritual notes which he wrote during this period seemed to indicate that his experience in prayer and in union with God was real and profound. But could one say that his professional life was also inspired by the spirit of the gospel? It was sometimes claimed, I do not know whether with truth or not, that he ran the Embassy in a manner that was almost military. Then during his retirement in Montreal from 1954 to 1959, he spent his days in the apartment on Sherbrooke Street, having few interests outside of his family and spiritual life; he spent a fair amount of time worrying about his health, and he suffered a great deal from the enforced idleness which he felt had been thrust upon him. But when he became Governor General, he threw open the windows of his spirit, and assumed a rôle which one might almost describe as benevolently paternal. He loved all Canadians without distinction of race, religion or ideal. He was interested in all, and in all their activities. He welcomed each letter which he received especially those asking for his help from someone in need or from some victim of injustice, and never did he fail to investigate their circumstances to see if he could help. In no sense did his professional life appear the least bit military. On the contrary at Rideau Hall, he created with my mother, a feeling of family, of confidence, of joy, of simplicity and of great goodwill.

In his relations with others my father seems to have found towards the end of his life a remarkable balance between his spiritual life, his simple but radiant capacity to give of himself and his undoubted sense of duty. As a young man he had shown himself to be a person of virtue and courage, with a clear sense of justice; later in life, his interior and spiritual life developed, and he became a man of prayer. Finally at Rideau Hall this interior life, rooted in his sense of justice, expanded into a simple and sensitive love for all men. He underlined in the writings of Charles de Foucauld[28] the passages where the author tells of his desire to be a "universal

---

[28] A Frenchman who lived as a hermit in the Sahara and died in 1916. In his youth a man of action, he became a man of prayer. One of the passages of his writings underlined by my father reads as follows: "Pray God that I be really a brother to all in this country. I would like all of them, Christians, Moslems, Jews and idolaters to see in me their brother, the universal brother." (*Itineraire Spirituel de Charles de Foucauld*, J.-F. Six, p. 274).

brother" a "brother to all men". At the end of his life, I think my
father aspired to just this.[29]

He had a special affection for children and for the humble and
those who suffered. We all remember examples of the way in
which he sought to bring whatever pleasure he could to those for
whom he felt a certain responsibility. For many years he visited
and helped the daughter of one of his former teachers, an old and
sick woman at the time he was Ambassador in Paris. At that same
period he made frequent visits to a former Embassy employee
dying of cancer in a Paris hospital, and he would go several times
a year to Chantilly to visit Father Gaume, a Jesuit who had been
his professor in Montreal and who was by then old and ill. He
would take infinite trouble if one of his friends or anyone employed at the Embassy fell ill to ensure that they had proper care
and would find some particular way to bring them pleasure. After
he had retired as Ambassador to France he frequently returned to
Paris. Each time he did so he would carefully prepare a list of those
people he wished most to see. Those who did did not know him well
would have been surprised to find that the first two names on his
list would inevitably be those of his former chauffeur and of a
Hindu who had been his masseur for a number of years. . . . He
did not have a good memory for names, but relied on my Mother's
uncanny ability in this field. But he did remember people and their
circumstances. If, when he met someone, he forgot to refer to some
member of their family or to some incident which he felt he should
have recalled, he would be angry with himself afterwards and
would take remarkable pains to repair his oversight. We would
often accuse him of going to too-great lengths to correct an omis-
sion we thought unimportant, but we would usually end up help-
ing him find the necessary telephone number or address so that he
could make good his lapse of memory.

He was extraordinarily generous with the limited amount of
money at his disposal. He would even give away funds which he
did not yet possess, relying on the indulgence of his bankers. The
number of those to whom he continuously and regularly gave help
is impressive—persons in need, missionary communities in India,
and the poor almost anywhere in the world. Sometimes we, his
children, were bold enough to suggest that some of those who
approached him for money were not genuinely in need, but he

[29] Father Legault in *La Presse* (Montreal), March 11, 1967, noted that my
father had "a sort of spiritual affinity with Charles de Foucauld, who called
himself the little brother of all men."

would reply with a disapproving look: "You may well be right, but it would be better to be abused than to fail to give to someone who is really in need."

It would be impossible to say too much about his love for the young, especially toward the end of his life. When with children he himself became a child. He loved to laugh with them, to play with them, and to tease them. Those of us who witnessed the event will not forget those wonderful afternoons at Rideau Hall during the Christmas season when underprivileged children were invited to a party. He would be surrounded, indeed buried by as many children as could get near him, to the delight of both host and guests! And he had a very special relationship with his small grandchildren, a sort of understanding that went much deeper than words.

My parents had a great gift for receiving and welcoming friends. They knew instantly how to put their guest at ease and to transform a function which might otherwise have been stiff and formal into a relaxed and happy occasion. They created between them a family spirit which gave warmth to every meeting. They conveyed a feeling of such genuine interest that each person felt free to express his innermost thoughts. For these reasons meetings and conversations with my parents were rarely superficial. The warmth and forthrightness of my father, linked with the vivacity and spontaneity of my mother, never failed to bring out the best in each of their guests.

My father had the true gift of friendship—or perhaps one should say he had developed and perfected those gifts which make a true friend. Many of those who had met him only once or twice felt nonetheless that they had established a deep and abiding friendship.

The following words come from a letter of sympathy after his death:

> ". . . But I think that General Vanier possessed the gift of making each one feel that he was their personal friend. He managed to convey this impression for the simple reason that it was true, every human being was precious to him!"[30]

"Augustin" in Le Devoir of March 8, 1967, expressed the feeling shared by so many others after meeting the Governor General:

> "You came away without having been subjected, at any moment, to that rather painful type of exhortation

[30] Letter from Gabrielle Roy, March 11, 1967.

which the elderly often peevishly extend to younger men. Rather it was that your own rôle in the solution of certain problems appeared in a clearer light, a more exacting perspective. When the time came to leave, you were offered a bed for the night but made to feel completely free to return to your own affairs. You were not made to feel that an honour had been extended to you, but rather were thanked for granting a favour to your hosts in coming to see them. The moment of separation did not mark a break in your relationship. It opened up a communion—this word with the word love summarizes the whole life of Georges P. Vanier—which was to become, in spite of yourself, a presence in your daily life, a gratuitous friendship, the source of which was to be found only in a spirit not of this world."[31]

Recently one of us heard someone in Quebec remark that after a conversation with the Governor General he felt proud to be a man. He added that my father had the rare gift of making another aware of his own worth or capabilities—in other words, of giving him strength and insight. Dr. Wilder Penfield said of him:

"With all that life brought him he never lost the common touch, the knack of friendship, the unfailing gift of understanding others. There was always time for laughter and companionship, and time for thought of the common good."[32]

"His was the gift of understanding," wrote Rabbi W. A. Wachsmann. "He sought to understand not only the will of the Creator but the ideas and aspirations and even the incoherencies of his fellowmen as well and to interpret them not from his, but from their point of view. . . ."[33]

He was always accessible, although this may sound strange in one who for many years had been in a position to be "protected" by his staff. His desire to deal personally with so many questions must have been a trial to those who worked with him, but it did allow him to keep in contact with a remarkable number of people. He gave many a new sense of security, a feeling that if the Gov-

[31] *Le Devoir*, Augustin, March 8, 1967.
[32] "Georges P. Vanier and Social Evolution", an address to the McGill Society of New York at the Princeton Club of New York, May 3, 1967.
[33] Regina *Leader-Post*, Sask., March 9, 1967.

ernor General were interested and involved in their problem, a solution would not be long in coming. He gave people the conviction that he cared, and gave such conviction to many who had long and painful experience of knowing what is genuine and what is not.

We have suggested that this flowering of love and understanding was the summit of the upward climb of his spiritual life, the fruit of years of practised virtue and prayer. He seems to have felt the full force of the words which Jesus spoke concerning love of one's neighbour, love which seems to be identical with the love of God and which stems from God's love. He had underlined the following passages in the autobiography of St. Thérèse of Lisieux.

> "The kingdom of heaven will not give entrance to every man who calls me Master, Master; only to the man who does the will of God, my Father."[34] What was this will of God? Jesus kept on telling us about that; you might almost say on every page of his gospel. But at the Last Supper . . . He gave them, this dear Redeemer of ours, a new commandment. He says to them—oh, so tenderly!—"I have a new commandment to give you, that you are to love one another; that your love for one another is to be like the love I have borne you. The mark by which all men will know you for my disciples will be the love you bear one another."[35]

In St. Bartholomew's Anglican Church in Ottawa, on November 15, 1964, my father said:

> "Of all the attributes of the spirit, the greatest is love. By this power the Good Shepherd and His flock know each other. From Him we have the two great commandments of love. Let us not be tempted to restrict these commandments to a narrow view of charity—namely love of one's neighbour only after providing for oneself. Charity in the Judaic tradition embraces justice, and this according to Plato is the virtue by which a man has and does all that rightly belongs to him. This activity of the whole man is the test of love. May our lives therefore be founded on love, and hallowed by prayer which is love's expression.
>
> We all need love—to give and to receive. It has been

[34] Autobiography of a Saint, Thérèse of Lisieux, p. 208, quoting Matt., 7, 21.
[35] John, 13, 34-35.

said that a mystic is a man who has fallen in love with God and that the first step to that state is prayer. We all have to fall in love with someone—why not God? And through him—with our neighbour."

At "Dorea", a home for delinquent children near Valleyfield, he said on May 13th, 1958:

"The scourge of this century, of our country—yes, of our country—at the moment is delinquency. What happens to the youngster without a home, living in the streets? He becomes a hooligan, a ruffian. And where does he end up? In prison. Well, Dorea takes in, safeguards and rehabilitates such youngsters and thus tries to stop the spread of the cancer of delinquency. What a work of salvation and redemption.

I admit that I am profoundly moved. This is hardly surprising, Reverend Father, since your account of the needs, problems and anguish of these forsaken children paints a staggering picture.

The complacent citizen who hears this, and we are all rather complacent my friends, must be worried, must find his conscience somewhat troubled. If we have a really Christian spirit we must ask ourselves—as you have suggested Reverend Father—what sort of welcome Christ will give us when we render our account. What will we say to Jesus when He asks 'And you, legitimate child, what have you done for your brother, he whom they call illegitimate? He is my child, just as legitimate and just as loved as you. What have you done for him?'

And we, the complacent ones, looking around that heaven for which we longed—always supposing we get there at all—will be surprised to see those illegitimate brothers occupying the best seats in the celestial amphitheatre! Those same brothers to whom we failed to teach the meaning of love, here below.

Do not think that I am speaking in this way in order to play on our emotions and sentimentality. No, it is simply in order to put ourselves face to face with our responsibilities which are immense. And in order to introduce an element of reality into our materialistic, superficial and selfish lives.

Why are we here, you and I? We are here to help complete this monument to faith, hope and charity that Father Lussier is building. His difficulties and his problems are great but so are his courage and love, for he is building to the glory of God and for forsaken children. And we will succeeed: we will carry through a meritorious action in the eyes of our fellow men and of Christ. You have done a good deed in coming this evening to support the efforts of Madame Leclair. Continue to help Dorea. In addition to giving, canvass your friends, get them interested in this work, make conversions.

Allow me to quote, with the greatest respect, a passage from the Gospel which can be applied to those who beg for gifts for Dorea. It is a passage which you know well; it teaches patience, perseverance, tenacity, obstinacy; the will never to accept a refusal to subscribe. Here it is:

Our Lord says:

'Let us suppose that one of you has a friend, to whom he goes at dead of night, and asks him, lend me three loaves of bread, neighbour; a friend of mine has turned in to me after a journey, and I have nothing to offer him. And suppose the other answers, from within doors: 'Do not put me to such trouble; the door is locked, my children and I are in bed; I cannot bestir myself to grant thy request.' I tell you, even if he will not bestir himself to grant it out of friendship, shameless asking will make him rise and give his friend all that he needs.'[36]

The point I am trying to make is that if at first your request is refused—which is unlikely—pretend not to understand, continue to ask. If necessary, be a nuisance, importunate, tiresome, aggravating, embarrassing, haunt your friends until they are worn out and give in just for a bit of peace!

But I know you will have little trouble in making your point. Why? Because our cause is magnificent, it speaks for itself.

Let us give and let us ask others to give. Let us get to work, never forgetting that no man is the poorer for giving to his brother for the love of God."

At a dinner given by the *Fondation de la Famille Terrienne*, in Montreal on February 8, 1964 he spoke as follows:

[36] Luke, 11, 5-9.

"Generosity seeks always to give, and to give not in any paternalistic manner, but through the inspiration of a genuine love, which inspires the giver to espouse both the joys and the suffering of others. If our blessings, which are the gifts of God and of Nature, are not placed in the service of others through love, we can be sure that our consciences will condemn us. We are all our brother's keepers for as long as poverty exists in our world and I do not speak only of material poverty, but also of spiritual, intellectual, cultural, psychological and even physical poverty, and such poverties will be always with us; so long as they exist, our compassion will not only involve us in the suffering of individuals, but will inspire us as well to create national and even international institutions to help supply a remedy. Only thus will we be able to build a society in which each person may find fulfillment, not only in the love of God, but also of his neighbour.

There are many ways in which we can practise generosity and witness before others to the happiness we ourselves possess. I am not thinking here only, or even primarily, of gifts of money; I am speaking first and foremost of gifts of the heart. Those who are in misery and those who suffer often have more need of affection and friendship than they have of money. In our age, when so many suffer from loneliness, especially perhaps in our larger cities, it is essential that our united and happy homes have sufficient compassion to open their hearts and their doors to those in need."

Speaking before the Catholic Hospital Association of Canada at the Château Laurier in Ottawa on May 18, 1964, he declared:

"When Jesus delivered his Sermon on the Mount, he saw in one beatific vision all the poor people of the world. He looked with special compassion not only on those who were poor through social circumstances, but also those made poor through physical inadequacies or suffering."

Speaking thus did my father have present in his mind the spirit of the text of the Gospel of St. Matthew:

"I was hungry and you gave me food, I was thirsty

and you gave me drink, I was a stranger and you welcomed me, I was naked and you clothed me, I was sick and you visited me, I was in prison and you came to me.... Truly, I say to you, as you did it to one of the least of these my brethren, you did it to me."[37]

In one of his spiritual notes dated January 1, 1955, my father wrote of the following events, which seem both full of mystery and yet radiant with sensitive spiritual teaching:

"Yesterday afternoon I went to the reception which H.E. Cardinal Leger gives on the first of the year. Afterwards, I did my half-hour in the Cathedral then, leaving by the side door, I looked for a taxi. As none passed I walked to Dorchester Street and waited on the corner. At the same time I said to Jesus that we would go together to find one. The wind was rather cold. A man, coming from the north, crossed the road. He was in rags. I had the impression that he would speak to me. He did, in fact, come towards me and asked me in English if I could give him a few cents to buy . . . something. I answered in French 'yes' and he said 'oh thank you' in a voice trembling with gratitude. As I had some change I took it out of my pocket and gave it to him . . . 'here is about 50 cents.' Again he thanked me with the same voice—and left me.

This morning I woke about 2 o'clock and was in a state of affective prayer. At a given moment I said to God the Father or to Jesus—'God, abide with me . . .' and I thought a lot about the beggar of the day before."

He wished to follow Jesus in his love for the poor, and in his dealings with them he showed a wonderful sensitivity and tact. They felt his love and loved him in return as the following words written by Marjorie Conners in "Unity" April, 1967 bears witness:

"FROM THE ARMY OF THE POOR

They have no voice, the poor,
No way of telling their sorrow
To Government House.
This space is their's, then.
Through someone
To whom they have confided

---

[37] Matthew, 25, 35-37, 40.

In the days since the General died,
It speaks
For the inarticulate.

When an international famous personage of great distinction dies, the press, radio, television and the pulpits are graphic with eulogies, this is to be expected, is right and, in some cases, the panegyrics are true. . . .

But there is another kind of eulogy, rare, and so unexpected it gives us much material for reflection. Since the late Governor General Georges P. Vanier died, scarcely a day has passed without one of the brigade of outcasts expressing his sorrow and sense of loss. Some of these are veterans of the 'Van Doos', others were in the Black Watch. To them His Excellency was just the General or the Chief; their loss is greater than one might suppose. In a callous world, it helps to reflect that someone in the high places is concerned, full of compassion and solicitude for the despised and rejected ones. The General was loved. He is mourned. He will not be forgotten.

One old 'rubby' (rubbing alcohol addict) with unsteady walk, shaking hands, and alcoholic tears, said, 'I pray God to give our Chief the best.' This is only one quotation. There are countless expressions of sorrow from those who are often classed as riff-raff, scum, the dregs of society, a disgrace to any civilized community, a scandal to visitors; but we must remember that their situation is not the fault of any particular section of society. Many of them have army pensions plus the old age pension.

Some of the old veterans bring pictures of the General torn out of newspapers they have retrieved from wastepaper baskets on the streets. I pretend I haven't already seen them all!

This house[38] has lost a great friend and supporter. Lost? Perhaps not. Maybe the General, in the Place Beyond, will remember us."

We are convinced that "the General in the place beyond" not only remembers but that his care will remain even more faithful and practical.

[38] This house refers to "Patricia House" in Montreal, of which Mrs. Conners was the director. Mrs. Conners died on Christmas day 1968 at Patricia House while serving a Christmas lunch to her beloved poor.

"Symbol of unity

This deep desire for brotherhood which my father felt expressed itself in a keen sense of the need for unity. He was convinced that the primacy of love itself called for unity. In the daily press he was referred to as "the symbol of unity", "the apostle of unity", "the Ambassador for unity". The Canadian Prime Minister, Lester B. Pearson declared in the House of Commons, March 6, 1967:

> "He had a passionate belief in his country, in its unity, in its destiny of true greatness based on enduring values on patriotic ideals which should be shared by all its citizens. He made Canada and its unity his own crusade, in every word he uttered, in every visit he made and on every occasion that he honoured with his presence."

And Quebec Prime Minister Daniel Johnson declared that the Governor General made himself "the untiring apostle of harmony among all Canadians."[39]

There are so many things which one might say about my father's desire to preserve the unity of his country; his final years were dedicated to help Canadians of different origins understand and appreciate each other. Others could write with more eloquence than I on this subject. His New Year's messages remain for us not only a political, but also almost a spiritual testament to the importance of unity.

In his New Year's message, 1961, he said:

> "In this age of motion and the machine if we can achieve a daily moment of quiet, say ten minutes, for reflection or meditation we may be able to find ways of living the precept 'Love thy neighbour as thyself.' This creates a spirit of confidence and serenity. Who knows whether this may not be the first step towards the road of friendship among nations and the achievement of 'Peace on earth to men of good will.' "

One might have spoken, also, of his wish to strengthen the family, that indispensable building brick of human society. He felt that so many destructive forces in our age were assailing family values. It was this conviction that inspired him, with my mother, to call an important conference on the family, which took place

[39] *Le Devoir*, March 6, 1967.

in Ottawa in 1964, and which led to the foundation of the Vanier Institute of the Family. He said in his New Year's message of 1965:

"Last summer we decided to organize at Rideau Hall, an ecumenical congress on the family. Here we met, with men and women of various beliefs, languages and professions. We prayed and studied together. And we are continuing to work in the perspective of unifying and reaffirming family life in Canada. We sought to bring back to memory the very appropriate message of St. Paul: 'There is a variety of gifts but the same Spirit; and there are varieties of service, but the same Lord; and there are varieties of working, but the same God who inspires them all in every one.'"[40]

My father was truly a man who sought to promote unity in every field of human endeavour. These words of Reverend John Gladstone, at Yorkminster Park Baptist Church in Toronto, March 30th, 1967 enlarge this point:

"We can go on to say that his goodness found expression in a spirit of reconciliation. The seventh beatitude of Jesus proclaims a blessing on the peacemaker: 'Blessed are the peace-makers, for they shall be called the children of God.' This soldier was a man of peace. He was a reconciler, determined to build bridges of understanding across the dividing chasms of ignorance and nationalism. . . .

He was also a reconciler in the realm of religion. . . . Our need today is not for the spirit of the Inquisition, but for the spirit of Calvary—a spirit of reconciling love, eager to pray and work and look for the reformation of all Churches, and their revival by the Spirit of the living God. . . ."

The source of this spirit of unity we find beautifully enunciated in this text by Catherine Doherty:

"He gave me a feeling of intense security, just by being who he was. He was to me symbol of unity, not only the unity of a country, which unity he desired with a flaming desire, but the very essence of the spirit of unity, which can only come from a man who is united to his God."[41]

[40] 1 Cor., 12, 4-6.
[41] *Restoration*, Combermere, Ontario, April 1967.

These extracts help us to understand the almost universal reaction inspired by my father's death:

"... the emotion caused by the death of Georges Vanier is almost self explanatory ... this man was above all a witness to the absolute."[42]

Claude Ryan probably expressed the feelings of most Canadians when he wrote:

"We mourn especially the great servant of the State, but above all we mourn the universal friend, the brother hidden behind the holder of the highest office in the land.
To meet this man, particularly towards the end of his life, was to feel oneself closer to God, to the God he was so eager to meet."[43]

[42] Emile Legault, C.S.C., in *La Presse*, Montreal, March 11, 1967.
[43] Claude Ryan: "The Late Georges P. Vanier", in *Le Devoir*, Montreal, March 6, 1967.

APPENDIX

It seems appropriate here to add a few extracts from certain speeches or public conferences which my father gave between 1942 and 1955, in which he alluded to the rôle of the spiritual in the temporal.

We begin by a talk he addressed as Commander of the military district of Quebec, March 8, 1942, to the troups assembled at Valcartier Camp, after a Mass which inaugurated a campaign against blasphemy.

"Do not blaspheme"

"First, let me remind you that I know only too well what blasphemy means. I did not spend four years in the trenches during the First World War without having the sadness and shame of hearing men blaspheme. Therefore, unfortunately, I know what I am talking about. I heard the names of God, of Jesus Christ, of the Blessed Virgin said in such a way as to make me shudder. I heard profaned the names of the sacred vessels used in the sacrifice of the Mass, the ciborium and even the tabernacle. How can one explain this sacrilege except by the intervention of Satan, who uses our faith and our knowledge of our religion to arm us against God?

I will always remember a certain evening, during a battle. With great difficulty we were moving in single file towards the front line. It was dark; shells were exploding around us. Suddenly I heard in the night the voice of a man blaspheming. This blasphemy, at a time when we were so close to death made me afraid: because blasphemy calls down the wrath of God. I managed to reach the man who was blaspheming and said: "What has Christ done to you my friend, that you should insult Him thus?" He trembled like a child and almost burst into tears. He had blasphemed without thinking, almost without knowing. Without thinking? Without knowing? In fact, most of those who blaspheme excuse themselves by saying they do it without thinking. As though one could forget!

Do we believe, yes, or no, that Christ suffered and died on the Cross for us? If we believe this, how can we forget it for even one moment, let alone to the extent of heaping further injuries upon Him who loved us to the point where he gave His life for us?

If I dared I would suggest this: after this, when you feel resentment and anger, and you blaspheme, try substituting the name of your father for that of Christ or the name of your mother for that of the Blessed Virgin. You will not be able do to so because your whole being will revolt against committing this unnatural crime. What are we to say then about a crime against heaven? Should we not thrust it aside with fierce determination? Crush it underfoot like some foul serpent?

I am happy to learn from your chaplains that very many of you assist at evening prayers. Prayer is the best weapon against blasphemy. Those who really pray cannot blaspheme, because the two are irreconcilable. Faced with the light of prayer, the devil flees to outer darkness.

Officers and non-commissioned officers, it is your duty to give a good example to your men.

Some people imagine that swear words and blasphemies confer a certain authority. What a mistake . . . the contrary is true. A leader's authority rests in the respect and confidence he knows how to inspire in his men; on the example he gives of a life without fear and beyond reproach.

For God's sake, in this holy time of lent, make the resolution to stop blaspheming and to stop your friends from blaspheming. In this way we will draw down God's blessing on our mission."

"Spirit in war"

Extracts from an address by Brigadier Georges P. Vanier, before the Canadian Club of Montreal, Monday, November 30, 1942.

"I know you will forgive me if I paraphrase part of an address which I gave some time ago, when presenting wings to air navigators. I said to them:

'You know the glory and the beauty of living amongst the stars, above the clamour of petty controversy and sordid meanness. Every man worthy of the name, who cannot follow your example, envies you and the noble part you play in the designs of Providence.

When fighting in far-off, war-clouded skies, you will be protecting those in this country who are dearest to you; you will be protecting them in such a way—no other way should satisfy a self-respecting Canadian—that they will not suffer the savage cruelty and shameful indignity with which the Nazis have branded the women and children of Europe. You have understood the great truth that to defend Canada *in Canada* means necessarily bloodshed here and misery for our people. The protection of this country is in other skies if we do not wish *our* skies to be aflame with enemy fire.

Remember always that in the darkest hour on earth or aloft, you will never be alone. You will feel the warmth of the Divine Presence if you ask for it. I make bold to say that in you God is proud of His Creation. Our faith in Him and in His power should be measureless when we recall there is a special Providence in the closing of a sparrow's wings. Intrepid airmen, in your travels through the skies, may God bless, guide and keep in full flight the wings you wear over your hearts.'...

Why do I speak to you of spirit or of spiritual values in war?

Because I believe deeply and sincerely that above all the forces of matter, above all the planes and ships, and tanks and guns 'spirit' as opposed to matter, is the most powerful weapon in our possession.

Because I believe that the Nazi doctrine from the very start was doomed to failure, built up as it was on a Pagan conception of life and on lies. Its teaching does not conform to the one thing which matters and the one thing which stands and will stand forever—truth. It is not possible to build on any other foundation—everything else is shifting sand.

Because I believe that we will be in a hopeless mess at the end of the war unless we shape our lives on moral standards, personal as well as national, higher than those in existence today.

Is our democracy strong enough in a spiritual sense? For years, for generations, we have heard that democracy is on trial. The fact that it has been on trial for so long is proof of its inherent strength, but it is not a guarantee that in the end, the prisoner at the bar will not be condemned. This war has brought to life the weak points of democracy, there are many and you know them all as well as I. The future of democracy is in our hands now, during the war. The ultimate remedy does not lie only in the building up of purely physical material forces and armaments: it lies also, and essentially, in a more rigid observance of our duties and obligations to God, country and fellow man; it lies also in the free acceptance of all sacrifices however painful, which a firmer moral code will impose. We shall have to forego many of our personal privileges and pseudo rights.

Some are beginning to realize that democracy, without a Divine core to reinforce it, will find it difficult, if not impossible, to weather the storm. The President of the United States, said, a short time ago: "We know that the spiritual liberties of mankind are in jeopardy—we are at war with the forces of evil abroad—we shall need all our spiritual resources to sustain us in the days to come. Providentially, there is always guidance if one knows where to look. Said the psalmist: 'Thy Word is a lamp unto my feet, and a light unto my path.'"

If we invited this Divine Guidance more often, the fog of doubt in which we live would be dissipated. . . .

Yes, we must have faith. Faith in God and his power to help. Faith in the righteousness of our cause; faith in ourselves and in the ultimate victory. The faith which moves mountains can work other miracles, and thus upset the natural orbit. 'More things are wrought by prayer than this world dreams of.' Would that we could return to the simple faith of our fathers, and that we could infuse into our daily lives belief in the power of prayer. Each one of us then would have within himself a source of Divine inspiration, which Hitler in his pagan conception of life, spurns!

There is a tendency, in some quarters, to associate the thought of spirit or prayer with weakness, as if one ceased to be a realist when praying. A great living scientist has written this: 'Today, as never before, prayer is a necessity in the lives of men and nations. The lack of emphasis on the religious sense has brought the world to the edge of destruction. Our deepest source of power and perfection has been left miserably undeveloped. If the power of prayer is again released and used clearly in the lives of common men and women, there is yet hope that our prayers for a better world will be answered.' Those of you who have read the Reader's Digest for November know who he is: the famous Dr. Carrel. . . .

Faith born of prayer leads naturally to charity, the greatest virtue of them all. And we must have charity if we hope to make a better world.

You remember the story of the lawyer who said to Jesus: 'And

54

who is my neighbour?' And Jesus answering said: 'A certain man went down from Jerusalem to Jericho and fell among robbers, who also stripped him and having wounded him went away, leaving him half dead. And it chanced, that a certain priest went down the same way, and seeing him, passed by. In like manner also a Levite, when he was near the place and saw him, passed by. But a certain Samaritan, being on his journey, came near him, and seeing him, was moved with compassion. And going up to him, bound up his wounds, pouring in oil and wine, and setting him upon his own beast, brought him to an inn and took care of him.'

It was on the road from Jerusalem to Jericho that the robbers stripped and wounded and left half-dead the poor traveller of the Gospel. But what of the millions who are being stripped, wounded and left half dead and dead on the blood-stained road from Rotterdam to Warsaw and Belgrade—on all the roads in tortured Europe. Is not each one of these our brother?

What is Christ to you and to me? Is He only a legend or a symbol of a page in history?

If He is more to us than this, if He lives in us, we must not, we will not, rest until these brothers of ours have been liberated.

Although my title limits me to a consideration of spirit in wartime, you will forgive me, I know, if I make a short incursion into the after-war period. . . . Frankly I am less afraid of the war than of the after war, and I believe most sincerely that spiritual factors if anything will be more essential then.

If we think that after the war we will be able to go on living in our old comfortable materialistic way, we are wrong. There is going to be a new order of things—through evolution if we are wise, through revolution otherwise.

If we do not put into practice now the teachings of Christ we shall find ourselves, when hostilities cease, faced with the dangers which spring from selfishness, envy, greed, hatred—vices which can be national as well as personal. It is no easy or trite commonplace to say that it will be easier to win the war than to establish a peace which will be based on justice. I share the view expressed in an article which I read recently in the Press. I quote: 'It seems to me that present problems—the bitter clash of political ideologies, racial hatred, the unspeakable horrors of war and the threat to our entire civilization—force us to admit that there is no solution for the world's ills except the practical application of the simple truths that were taught to poor fishermen and the Jewish peasants by one who, 1900 years ago, was crucified.'

I am sure that the war will bring us to our knees in prayer, but if it does not, the cataclysm which follows the war will surely do so.

In conclusion, let me reaffirm that I do not advocate as a means to victory, faith, prayer and charity, coupled with complacency. Heaven forbid. But I do believe profoundly, that the man who receives help from above is better fitted to accept responsibility, better armed for the combat. The man who believes that he will live until God's appointed time has come will face danger, serene and unafraid. Julian Grenfell, killed in action in 1915, gave true expression to this feeling of serenity, when he wrote thus of the soldier in battle:

> 'And when the burning moment breaks
> And all things else are out of mind
> And only joy of battle takes
> Him by the throat, and makes him blind,
>
> Through joy and blindness he shall know
> Not caring much to know, that still
> Nor lead nor steel shall reach him, so
> That it be not the destined will.'

Let us begin now to associate prayer with power, faith with fire, charity with clear swift action. May these spiritual shafts shatter the clouds of doubt and fear, light our path through the dark valley of war and guide us, however cruel the road, to the Mount on which 19 centuries ago a certain Sermon was preached."

"Our World has an urgent need for a spiritual élite"

In the following talk my father described, as he saw it, the rôle of France in spiritual and religious domains. He spoke before an audience of professors and students of the Institut Catholique in Paris on November 26, 1952.

"What is it that our world needs at this moment before anything else, and needs with pressing urgency? Our world needs a soul, it needs a spirit. Our universe is being transformed into a sort of immense machine, the working of which is becoming more and more complicated and oppressive. The world we know has turned into a giant, no longer to be measured in human terms. The conflicts between nations and especially the wars of today, which are in part a result of economic crises and in part an expression of the passions and ambitions of men, are the dominant contributing factors to this dehumanization. Bombardments destroy entire cities which took centuries to build, cities which in the different styles of their buildings had preciously maintained and blended an entire heritage rich with a variety of human values which found expression there. These cities, the appearance of which evoke all the history of a people and preserved for future generations an inestimable educational potential, are now being thoughtlessly demolished and replaced by uniform constructions representing only one moment in history and often only one type of architecture. The old towns which used to be so different from each other have now become modern cities which, no matter what country in which they are found, all too often look exactly alike.

Our world stands in need of an accelerated development of virtually all qualitative values. Only the spirit can bring this element of qualitative value. Technology by itself is incapable of doing so. And, it must be added that our world, which not only unceasingly grows larger but which more and more conforms on a quantitative plane, has need of parallel unity on the qualitative and spiritual plane.

What sort of spiritual development does our modern world need? Will spiritual values, to repeat a term which has often been used, be sufficient in themselves to re-establish balance and harmony in our universe? I think not and I believe that as Catholics we must have the magnanimity to concede that our world needs not just 'spiritual values' but *genuine* spirituality, the only spirituality deserving of the name, that of the Holy Spirit. Man's intellect left to itself is incapable of creating unity in this immense universe. The giant is too big to be formed and unified by man's intellect alone. God must give us His Spirit and man must transcend himself to participate in the Spirit of the Almighty.

Man's intellect can, no doubt, develop to a fine art his understanding of our world of human realities, of sociology and history. But once having analysed, the powers of the human intellect are much more limited when it comes to synthesizing, to re-uniting. Certainly, the intellect can accomplish partial synthesis, but it remains incapable of achieving the total re-uniting. Man's intellect, left to its own resources, cannot even accomplish unity among economical and social forces or harmony between them and the sphere of our personal values. In the little world which is each one of us, our powers of reason are incapable of establishing perfect unity between knowledge and technical abilities on the one hand, and love and sentiments on the other. For that matter, to establish unity around us, to carry unity and therefore peace to others we must be in a state of peace and harmony ourselves. A man divided within himself can sow only the seeds of disunity and war. Only the Spirit of God, Creator of both matter and spirit, source of both truth and love, can bring harmony from such diversity. Our world longs for this vital and profound unity, for we know that without it we will perish.

Our world has an urgent need for a *spiritual élite*. But we can and must be even more precise than that, for the world needs above all an *élite of God*, an élite of spiritually minded men of God, who have been formed by God, who have been students in God's school and who, thereafter, are able to radiate His Spirit. These spiritually minded men of God are the friends of God, those with whom God has entered into intimate contact, whom He makes a part of His Spirit. They are the contemplatives and the saints. It is they who must bring to our world this qualitative element, this factor of indispensable unity so that the world may find harmony therein.

I have said that France is the country of the spirit and of spirituality. Can I now be more precise and say that France is the land of saints? Can we not claim that the saints of France like all the other saints, are above all the friends of God, and moreover, that they are numbered among the most magnificent figures in French history since they give the best image of the particular genius of their country.

I am thinking of St. Louis, of St. Vincent de Paul, of St. François de Sales, of Joan of Arc, of St. Margaret-Mary . . . and those closer to our times, St. Bernadette, the shepherdess of Lourdes, of the Curé d'Ars, of St. Louis Marie Grignion de Montfort, of the young Sister Thérèse, to mention only those who have been canonized.

May I add one word to complete my thesis? France is the land of saints, but only because it is the land that Mary, the Queen of saints, seems to have loved with a particular fondness. By the vow of Louis XIII, this kingdom was entrusted to her or rather it was given to her. The Feast of the Assumption, the feast of the Coronation of Mary, has since that time been specially celebrated in France. Mary is called the "Queen of France", and in recent centuries, the Blessed Virgin has seemed particularly fond of visiting this country. She appears almost at home in France, a country which seems to have been selected as the site for her earthly appearances. Mary came to la Salette, to Pontmain, to Lourdes . . . and by doing so, she seems to wish to recall to the people of France and indeed to all people that they must draw near to her if they are to let God give them His Holy Spirit and make of them His Saints.

At the dawn of modern times, before the successive wars which racked Europe, the Blessed Virgin came to remind us that the only way to regain our equilibrium was to be found not in science or technology, nor even in philosophy, but only in the simplicity of the Gospel, the fruit of the spirit and the gift of God.

Young French men and women, who are privileged and fortunate to receive your training here: I would that these few words may show you reasons for great hope; reasons too why you should be happy to live in this 20th century. For a Christian, it is always the present moment which is the best; but more than this: these times—because they contain a tragic element—can be fruitful in the grace of saintliness. You must be magnanimous in your hope so as to see clearly the depth and breadth of your vocation.

Yes be magnanimous, because you bear two proud titles: you are French and you are Catholic. You are an élite not only of the spirit but of the soul and such an élite always succeeds in breaking through in the end and imposing itself on the nation. Your presence and your work are essential for the life of France and for humanity.

I sometimes hear complaints and cries of distress because we no longer live "in the good old times" . . . Come on . . . the good time is now, magnificent, apocalyptic, on God's scale: a time of struggle between good and evil, a time for decision, and in which there is no place for the lukewarm and the coward.

Oh, how St. Paul would have loved to live today. Can you not hear his message? the same after 19 centuries?

> "I have no more to say, brethren, except this: draw your strength from the Lord, from that mastery which his power supplies. You must wear all the weapons in God's armoury, if you would find strength to resist the cunning of the devil. It is not against flesh and blood that we enter the lists: we have to do with princedoms and powers, with those who have mastery of the world in these dark days, with malign influence in an order higher than ours. Take up all God's armour, then; so you will be able to stand your ground when the evil time comes, and be found still on your feet, when all the task is over. Stand fast, your loins girt with truth, the breast-plate of justice fitted on,

and your feet shod in readiness to publish the gospel of peace. With all this, take up the shield of faith, with which you will be able to quench all the fire-tipped arrows of your wicked enemy: make the helmet of salvation your own, and the sword of the spirit, God's word."[1]

"The role of the contemplative in the world"

At the time he was Canadian Ambassador, my father gave the following talk to Trappist monks at the Abbey of Bellefontaine near Angers, France.

Ever since their eldest son had entered the Trappist Monastery at Oka in 1947, our parents had felt a strong bond uniting them to this monastic order consecrated to a life of silence, prayer and manual work. They felt that the vocation of their son was a special mark of God's goodness towards them.

In the talk, my father outlined the rôle of the contemplative and mystic in the modern world. This was no abstract idea or notion divorced from reality. He was so convinced of what he affirmed that, during a great part of his life, and in particular as Governor General, he remained in close touch with men and women of prayer, with monasteries and carmelite convents, and always asked for the help of their prayer.

"... You know, I am sure, the bonds which unite me so intimately to your Order, bonds of country and a personal bond. For the Abbey of Notre Dame du Lac at Oka in Quebec is happy and honoured to have been founded by you. A few days ago I wrote to the Most Reverend Dom Pacôme, whom you know well, to tell him of my coming visit to Bellefontaine and said that, on his behalf, I would bring you a message of filial friendship. So you will understand when I say I feel at home here—almost one of the family.

I want to take this opportunity of telling you what you represent for us in the world. I come to you as a beggar, begging prayers, contemplation, sacrifice, for myself, for my country, for the world.

Contemporary society has implicit in its administrative structure a materialism which is—so it seems to me—the greatest danger we face today.

[1] Holy Bible, Knox translation: Ephesians 6, 10-17.

60

The world has developed considerably in recent years, but this has been a superficial development, a material development. . . . Man can extend the exploitable part of the universe; he can increase productivity by perfecting his tools and making better use of raw materials. It has been said very truly that man created nothing when he discovered atomic energy; he merely unleashed unsuspected natural forces by his technology. Has he unleashed these forces for good or for evil? The Creator had kept them hidden, making use of them in the framework of great cosmic phenomena. Their potential seems outside the human scale—too great for the intelligence of man; an intelligence so fertile in the domain of science and technology but so limited in comprehending ultimate reality.

The heart of man, enslaved by egoism and passion, is no better prepared to bear the burden of this new power.

I leave these problems to philosophers and theologians, but I feel one must avoid two extremes, on the one hand a pessimism which sees in material civilization only the work of the devil, and on the other a facile optimism which denies the real problems posed by material progress.

A simple Christian who thinks about the present state of the world in the light of his faith, is horrified to see men who, almost in a frenzy, are developing scientific knowledge and technology, and who are at the same time oblivious to the contemplative aspect of intelligence. The more they apply themselves to the means, the more they forget the ends.

You may think me a pessimist. No, that is not a Christian attitude and, thank God, so far I have been spared this temptation. For the Christian the period in which he lives is always the best since this is God's good pleasure for him.

But let me tell you why I feel this confidence. I feel it because of *you*, because of all contemplative souls; *they* are reasons for shunning pessimism and inviting confidence.

If one were to see only the material development of the world, one could easily feel great anguish. But hope springs again when one considers the modern world with all that it represents, including that invisible world, sensed only occasionally in time and place. God allows an awareness of this hidden world to comfort us . . . think of the growth of the Cistercian order in North America in particular . . . this, surely, is a sign that God is not abandoning the world but that He cares for us.

There are all those souls, chosen by God, living solitary contemplative lives, isolated from the world. But particularly there are contemplative communities who live their contemplative lives integrated in society. By their monasteries, their mode of life and their religious profession which is a public act, such men of God, like other men, are part of our world and are as it were its centre of gravity.

Action depends on contemplation, which is the source and also the end of action. This metaphysical law is brought out strikingly by Our Lord in the Gospels. It is a law of divine government, valid therefore at all times and in all places. When there are no more contemplatives here below the world will vanish. It will have lost in the eyes of God its true significance. The man of action will destroy himself if he loses sight of his goal and the means of attaining it.

·But this principle can be realized in many different ways. Today action has developed horizontally out of all proportion, and in so doing it has become not only de-spiritualized but de-humanized. In order to maintain the vertical axis, as it were, and restore the balance of the world God seems to have intensified the contemplative life: the number of contemplative vocations is increasing and such souls seem guided towards an ever holier, purer form of contemplation, of which the Holy Sprit only is the Master.

In a world where specialization is the order of the day, God Himself seems to want to specialize. You know what I am trying to say: at the height of the middle ages, the sons of St. Benedict performed many functions both in the Church and in the world: they cleared the forests, they were apostles and catechists as well as being contemplatives. Later, God inspired the formation of other Orders specializing in apostolic work and works of mercy. More recently the Holy Spirit has inspired the formation of Catholic action groups so that laymen may assist the clergy in their work.

The greater the tendency of the world to specialize and exteriorize, the greater the tendency for it to be oppressed by its own riches, the more does the Holy Spirit desire contemplatives, free and pure by reason of their poverty, the more does He wish them to be hidden and the more does He ask of them lives of sacrifice and renunciation.

Although the world lacks adequate human insight, God seems to be deepening the world of contemplation which is the hidden source of our universe but which nonetheless forms its solid foundation. Inspite of the appalling frailty of man's political structures, such contemplative institutions form a backbone which can, if God so wills, maintain the stability of the world. Renewal remains possible as long as citadels of contemplation, such as those of the cistercians, continue their pure hidden sacrificial lives. Their presence indicates that the recuperative power of the world is there, unbroken. The world still has a heart which can, if God wills, renew all things.

I would like to mention an example which concerns your monasteries in particular, where modern techniques are in fact employed with their true end in view. I am told that during this summer certain of your monasteries have been able to say the Divine Office with greater solemnity, to maintain longer hours of prayer and study thanks to new harvesting machines. These machines allowed the friends of Jesus to remain close to Him in prayer for a longer time; the machines made it possible for more prayer and contemplation to rise from our poor world. Thus, it seems to me, these machines have been put to the use which should be theirs: that is to serve the servants of God.

You understand now what we ask of you. First, that you remain close to God, that you specialize more and more (if you will allow such an expression) in your contemplative lives. Plunge yourselves ever deeper into the Heart of Jesus so that through your prayer and the Divine Office, God will remain ever present in the world, and your hearts become more and more receptacles for Divine Love. This is your first and unique mission.

In remaining close to God you draw down His blessings on us all. And you are, day and night, in close proximity to the Queen of Heaven; you never leave the walls of her palace since Mary is crowned Queen of each of your monasteries. Ask her, therefore, at all times by your very presence, to give light and strength to your brothers who lead a life of action; they need this help in the maelstrom of activity and movement and when, faced with pressing problems, they forget to turn to God.

That which we omit to do in the world we can do through you our brothers, friends of God. The Communion of Saints is so consoling in this context. When one is committed to action, as I am, and knows that a word said at an official reception without much thought, or when one is tired and therefore careless, may influence men of state, it is good to be able to lean on the silence of contemplatives. It is good to know at such times that men of God to whom we are profoundly united are silent in the presence of Jesus and Mary and can obtain for us the gift of counsel to enlighten us.

That is why, before leaving you, I want to repeat that my wife and I come to you as beggars, for ourselves and those dear to us and also for all those committed to a life of action. The one favour we ask of you is to consider us as part of your family and keep us in your prayer and contemplation."

Here are some extracts from a talk on "The man of government" given in France (1953) and again in Canada (1955).

". . . What should be the essential attributes of the man called to a political life? What attributes will make of him a great statesman, not only as history sees him but also, I suggest, in the eyes of God?

Should they be primarily intellectual qualities? . . . knowledge of science? . . . knowledge of philosophy? . . . knowledge of history? Certainly a vast intellectual culture is necessary, particularly in the field of history. But pure philosophers and, I think, also pure historians are not good men of government. It seems that philosophy and history are not the disciplines through which they should form their basic outlook, their fundamental attitudes.

Are technical aptitudes required then? Certainly an efficient administration is a source of strength, but an efficient administration can serve an unjust cause. Administration, from the technical point of view, is considered perfect when each file is up to date, nothing is missing, order reigns supreme. But administrative order is not universal order and it can in fact serve a more profound disorder such as social injustice or religious persecution.

Modern technology places remarkable resources in the hands of a country's leaders. Such resources are merely instruments and can be used for good or for evil. Will they be used to further peace and justice or war and oppression? An administration itself is no more than an instrument. It needs a head, a heart and a will—in a word it needs a person, conscious, free and in possession of certain moral attributes: prudence and justice and all the other virtues which ensure integrity and harmony. These are the essential, primordial qualities of a man of government. Such a leader may lean heavily on the advice of scientists and technologists for historical and theoretical knowledge and for the most efficient use of the resources at his disposal. But if he is to seek their advice with impartiality and accept it, even when it conflicts with his own ideas, prejudices and temperament, he must be humble, modest, prudent, just . . . and in terms of these moral attributes no one can replace him, for these are essentially personal qualities.

64

Technology and specialization are indispensable but they should be tools used by true leaders whose spirit and heart are directed toward the ultimate good of their country. This ultimate good, since it belongs to the moral order, goes beyond country and should therefore permit true collaboration between the nations of the world; a collaboration based on faith and justice and not just a compromise without sincerity and equity.

These moral attributes are the mark of the true leader and they alone are a guarantee of his capacity to assume responsibility.

But can we stop there? Morality finds stability and more particularly inspiration and strength in religion. This is true of personal morality but even more so for the morality of government which is more complex and difficult. The morality of government demands greater insight because its range of action is wider. An international morality deprived of its religious foundations becomes vague and hesitant. Almost inevitably it lacks dynamism and strength.

In any event, for the man of faith, morality has its foundation and its finality in religion.

If all the moral virtues are necessary for the proper functioning of just and prudent government, surely the Christian must see that the theological virtues are also necessary—are in fact even more necessary. Government, as we have seen, is of a higher order than technology and must regulate its use. It lies in the realm of morality. But morality itself is subordinate to religion and faith. If the man of government is to maintain and develop all that is required for the common good of his country it is imperative that he be aware of the need to subordinate this to God Himself.

Surely it is a matter of urgency today that men who believe in Christ, and who count their faith above all things, should unite in order to overcome, not only the limitations of their own egoism but even that of their country, and thus help each other and save what remains of Christianity in the world.

It is undoubtedly a delicate matter to speak of 'Christian government'—the term is open to misinterpretation—but it is absolutely necessary that government by Christians draw inspiration from their faith. It is indispensable today that men of government possess sufficient magnanimity and faith to consider the common good of their country in a wider perspective, as subordinate to the universality of the Christian faith.

We must never forget that the supreme goal of society is to establish the greatest possible friendship among men. For the Christian, perfect friendship is to love and this love is embodied in Christ. Certainly the common good of the city and of the state is, in itself, good. Civic friendship is a human reality and distinct from a love flowing directly from God, but it would seem that such friendship cannot survive separated from this Divine Love.

Given the nature of political life and the exigencies of service therein, should not the man of government be also a man of prayer?

It has been said often enough that the management of public affairs is a difficult matter, particularly in these days. The moral qualities required are particularly difficult for the man of government to attain: he cannot live like a monk, his duties require him to live in the world—in the midst of the most seductive and dangerous aspects the world has to offer. He needs prayer to strengthen his faith and to ensure that this faith permeates his whole life and particularly his political life. How could he, by the sole use of his own reason and will, preserve a sense of the ultimate finality of his country? How can he have sufficient magnanimity and courage to rise above the interests of his own country when it is a question of respecting the rights of others and particularly of working for the good of Christianity.

In the world of today human wisdom, left to its own resources, is incapable of finding satisfactory solutions let alone of achieving them. The Christian knows that, among the gifts of the Spirit, that of counsel is given in order to counterbalance, in difficult situations, the defects of prudence, personal prudence and prudence in government. The Spirit thus allows us to share in the Wisdom of God Himself, Who enlightens us and guides us in the making of practical decisions.

If the man of government lives as a friend of God, if he has at heart the maintenance of a true intimacy with Him, if by his interior life he is united to Jesus Christ, then it seems that he can expect the Holy Spirit to help him remain in the path of integrity, justice, prudence and wisdom in government. For, let us not forget it, the Holy Spirit is Master, not only of spiritual but also of material reality. . . ."

66